John V. Pavlik

PUBLIC
RELATIONS

What Research Tells Us

Volume 16. The Sage COMMTEXT Series

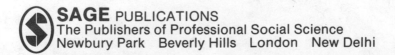

SAGE PUBLICATIONS
The Publishers of Professional Social Science
Newbury Park   Beverly Hills   London   New Delhi

For information address:

SAGE Publications, Inc.
2111 West Hillcrest Drive
Newbury Park, California 91320

SAGE Publications Inc.
275 South Beverly Drive
Beverly Hills
California 90212

SAGE Publications Ltd.
28 Banner Street
London EC1Y 8QE
England

SAGE PUBLICATIONS India Pvt. Ltd.
M-32 Market
Greater Kailash I
New Delhi 110 048 India

Printed in the United States of America

Library of Congress Cataloging-in-Publication Data

Pavlik, John Vernon.
    Public relations.

    (The Sage commtext series ; v. 16)
    Bibliography: p.
    Includes index.
    1. Public relations--Research. 2. Communication--
Research. I. Title. II. Series.
HM263.P36   1987   659.2'072   87-13200
ISBN 0-8039-2950-1
ISBN 0-8039-2951-X (pbk.)

CONTENTS

FOREWORD

Few would believe how much of the "news" we receive and use in our lives is a "product" prepared by PR specialists for media outlets. Fewer still would believe how this private enterprise really works.

What do we really know about the nature, shape, and effect of the information packaged by PR people that is transmitted by journalists to the American public as news? That is the subject of this text, which relates what current research tells us about this unusual state of affairs.

Research into communications is by definition a dicey gamble. Those who pursue the task of thinking about thinking share with the PR researcher the inherent obstacle of dissecting an object that is used to figure out how to dissect the object. As Professor Pavlik aptly explains, the essence of the effort is to find the linkage between information, attitude, and behavior. Of these, only the last may be truly observed. Therefore, the rest of the process is largely determined by the communications theory of the observer. It is probably not remarkable that most researchers—academics and practitioners— have made research discoveries that fit comfortably with their philosophies. And there are many theories about how information works.

How do we know what is a "pseudo-event," in Dr. Daniel Boorstin's view, or what is real? How can we determine what is cognitive, or affective, from the subjective view of those who receive, process, and use information—the PR targets? What is the difference between "awareness" and "credibility" as objectives in a PR campaign, and how can you tell if one, but not the other, is achieved? How can we know, after the application of what is believed to be a very effective PR campaign, that the needle moved? Can the human use of information be studied as in a laboratory experiment? In fact, can the variables be identified or placed in a hierarchy, as a human being uses information to receive, process, shape attitude, or modify behavior? These are questions addressed by the text you are about to read.

It would be a convenient but perhaps boring world if the questions posed above were answerable somewhere in this text. True to life, the author raises what is known, or thought to be known, from research (and how it was known and from what research), leaving the rest to the reader. This is surely as it should be, because human understanding in this area is comparable to the place where Plato was interpreting shadows on the cave walls. In short, this text is a good place to start.

It's more than a start. Professor Pavlik raises the question of the objective of a PR program—a rather important thing to know if the intent is to research the *result*. Study of the political campaign has been more productive than study of the PR campaign to measure the direct relationship of propaganda to behavior. Professor Pavlik also investigates the role of the PR agent as flak or counselor, a matter determined in most cases more by the "needy" psychology of subservience than its practitioners would probably like to admit. This book incisively asks, "What are we observing?" in PR research: information reception, information processing, information utilization, or behavior? Or the connection between and among these functions? And, how do we know we have found something when something is found?

When we research the human use of information, are we delving into science or dabbling in art? How far, if anywhere, have PR researchers gotten in answering any of the relevant questions? And can any of this be quantified?

Marshall McLuhan claimed to be more intrigued by the properly put question than the perfectly put answer. When something is perfectly unknown, the best way to proceed is with "probes," some very thoughtful, others that may be speculative. But it's all there.

Once and for all, the idea of "qualitative" or nonsystematic research in communications is belittled, as it should be. This text shows conclusively that truly qualitative research is in fact systematic and that systems of collection and analysis can be applied to subjective, anecdotal, casual, or personalized findings relating to communications phenomena. Alternatives are a display of laziness or ignorance.

Positioning in the news medium itself is often analogous to positioning in the brain of the target receiver. Awareness and credibility, as characterizations of *received* information, must be carefully studied as to source, framing, and delivery, if we are to understand the difference between the role of advertising and that of public relations, especially if both are simultaneously used for the same purpose. Quantitative measures that invite separable features of communications effects or behaviors are therefore not only warranted, but invited. Many meaningful advances in this innovative area are cited in the text.

Central to the measure of public relations is the highly disputed issue about the role of propaganda: Does it put new, determining information in the heads of the targets, or does it simply reorganize what is already there, with few if any additions to the information base? Research to date has centered largely on the first thesis, the educational thrust, of propaganda; as time proceeds, perhaps the second, and more fruitful, area will be opened to inquiry.

As always a book on communications research discusses what is known about the observations of human communications. Scientific inquiry seeks a case in which the laboratory can control all but one variable, a human situation most likely to be found in a morgue. In human communications, nothing is fixed and the weight of variables is also a variable in time; so, therefore, the way to learn is by a cut through the existing flux. In political campaigns, for example, tracking polls that reach back to a baseline poll, in comparison to a continuing content analysis, can tell the story of what went out, what was received, (marginally) how it was received or processed, and what behavior should occur as a result. Election statistics and election-day polls can shed additional light on what happened and why it happened. The application of what is known about the American political campaign to what is not known about the U.S. public relations campaign, therefore, is probably the field in which the next steps in research—and under-standing—will take place, when we consider the matter Professor Pavlik has undertaken to describe in the admirable text that now follows.

—*Michael Rowan*
President, Strategic Information
Research Corporation
Former President,
International Association of
Political Consultants

PREFACE

The purpose of this book is to provide a portrait of the field of public relations based on evidence of systematic research. The view of the media—such as newspapers, magazines, and television—or support systems—such as advertising and public relations—that comes from research as opposed to descriptive impressions can be quite powerful.

Written primarily for undergraduates, this book reviews selected findings of research from a variety of research traditions and methodologies. Its scope is limited largely to those investigations conducted in the specific context of public relations. Of course, much research in such related fields as business, economics, and sociology, as well as social psychology, is pertinent to any understanding of public relations, but that is well beyond my scope. This book is intended to supplement, not to replace, the leading PR texts, including those with a strong research component (e.g., Cutlip, Center, & Broom's *Effective Public Relations*; Grunig & Hunt's *Managing Public Relations*).

The book provides a conceptual map of the field of public relations based on the best available scholarly information. The mapping here takes the form of a lively bibliographic essay, with some strong research summaries and quotes from key researchers and commentators to give the flavor of this diverse and fascinating work. In the pages that follow, more than 300 researchers who have conducted systematic, scholarly studies of public relations are cited. There are also occasional commentaries from practitioners who, although they may not be researchers, have some cogent insights about the value of PR research.

The idea of this book is to isolate in a useful fashion what extant scholarly research tells us about public relations, not to provide a complete portrait of all that is known about public relations.

Beginning with a review of what has been written and why, the book offers a broad brush of the field. This introduces several important questions for which the book seeks answers, including: What is the nature of research on public relations? What are its major themes? What was the motivation of the researchers? What did they hope to learn? What methods did they use? What was the yield of their studies?

Beyond this the book looks at the insights of scholarly information, distinguishing it from common-sense impression. For example, few students realize the major role that PR activities have in shaping the nature and content of today's news media. Scholarly research, however, tells us that PR activities—such as press conferences, news releases, and media events—often have a significant effect on the content of the media. This effect is called agenda setting.

Every field of research is defined not only by its scholarly literature, but also by its omissions and gaps. Thus the book asks, What have researchers failed to study? What are the holes in existing research-knowledge? Finally, there is a view of the emerging paradigm of PR research and theory, which suggests that something new is in the air, that the field is changing.

I wish to thank Professors Glen M. Broom, James E. Grunig, Charles T. Salmon, and Daniel B. Wackman for their assistance while I was developing this book. A special thanks to Michael Rowan, president of Strategic Information Research Corporation for his contribution to this book.

—John V. Pavlik
University of Pennsylvania

INTRODUCTION

Research on public relations falls into two broad classes: that conducted in the public domain, and that conducted in the private domain. Public domain research is just that—publicly available in visible places for the asking or for a price. Private domain research is proprietary, typically conducted for business or other private sources, and generally not accessible to the public.

Research in the public domain is often produced by persons in university settings. It is likely to deal with broad issues such as trends in public relations or roles of practitioners in public relations. For example, one of the first articles on public relations (Bernays, 1937) was entitled "Recent Trends in Public Relations Activities." The findings of such research are typically disseminated through academic journals and conferences. The Bernays's article, for instance, was published in the first issue of the *Public Opinion Quarterly*.

My concern in this book is with research that is widely available to the public—professors, practitioners, or students. Every study cited in this book is available for the reader's firsthand examination. If you have an interest in a particular study, you will typically find it available at a university or community public library.

One area of public research that I do not extensively review here is that conducted in governmental settings. Much research about government public relations does appear in standard, publicly available journals, however, and I do review key research—such as U.S. Census or industrial data sources, when relevant.

A considerable portion of the research on public relations has been conducted in private, corporate, or agency settings. Most of this industry research is proprietary in nature, meaning that the findings are confidential and not typically available to the public. There are many reasons for maintaining this confidentiality, including a concern over how other organizations might use this information.

Occasionally, corporate research is made public. For example, in 1977 James E. Grunig and Richard S. Franzen teamed up to discuss publicly the PR evaluation process at the Bell System. Grunig is a professor of public relations at the University of Maryland, while Franzen is the Director of Public Relations at the Bell System. They first presented their research at a measurement symposium, and later their findings were published in *Public Relations Review* (Franzen, 1977; Grunig, 1977).

Proprietary research is also sometimes released for publicity purposes. Miller Brewing, Co., for instance, sponsored a major investigation into America's interest and involvement in sports. This sports report was released to the public through the media and generated considerable publicity for the sponsor.

WHO CONDUCTS RESEARCH ON PUBLIC RELATIONS

Most of the published research on public relations has been conducted by academicians. A comprehensive literature review conducted for this book shows that four of five authors of systematic research on public relations are social scientists in academic settings. This includes faculty members at universities and colleges, as well as graduate students working toward master's and doctoral degrees. A review of the PR literature of the past 10 years confirms this, as more than 80% of the authors of research articles on public relations are associated with universities.

Leading academic researchers in the field of public relations include James Grunig, Glen M. Broom, David M. Dozier, William P. Ehling, Donald K. Wright, Carolyn G. Cline, and others. Most of these researchers have experience both in professional practice and in higher education. Broom, for example, had extensive professional experience in PR agency work before pursuing an academic career full time.

While the majority of these "PR scientists" are found in schools of journalism or communication, many teach in such related fields as sociology, psychology, business, or marketing. Some have the title "Professor of Public Relations," but for many, scholarship in public relations is not their full-time vocation. Maxwell McCombs, for instance, is primarily a professor of newspaper research, but has contributed much to our understanding of the effects of public relations through agenda-setting studies that posit that the media influence our perceptions of important public issues.

The research of McCombs (e.g., 1977) is also illustrative of the scholarly nature of this body of academic research. It is more and more designed to build theory about public relations, to help describe, explain, and predict the process and effects of public relations in society.

Academic scholars are likely to disseminate their findings through a variety of channels. A study that I conducted with two colleagues is illustrative. As graduate students at the University of Minnesota in the late 1970s, we studied the readership of employee newsletters at a major corporation. We wrote a paper describing our study, which was presented at the 1980 annual convention of the Association for Education in Journalism (now the Association for Education in Journalism and Mass Communication—AEJMC). Subsequently, this paper was published in *Public Relations Review,* a refereed research journal (Pavlik, Nwosu, & Gonzales, 1982). Studies by academics are also disseminated informally as working papers, pamphlets, and lectures before taking on a more formal appearance as monographs, articles, or books.

As indicated earlier, some studies pertaining to public relations are conducted by government researchers. They are often interested in tracking public opinion or studying the effects of public information campaigns. I will review landmark studies from governmental sources. PR practitioners also produce much of the research on public relations, although a large portion of this research remains in the private sector. This research is typically of an "applied" nature, dealing with specific problems or methods. Its purpose is often to develop a set of recommendations for or proposed solutions to some issue or problem. It is also used as a method for monitoring the environment and obtaining feedback from important publics.

Many different types of organizations, such as corporations or nonprofit organizations, conduct PR research.

Often the research is administered or overseen by someone directly involved in public relations, such as the PR director, a researcher in a corporate PR department, or a public information or public affairs officer in a government or university setting. On many occasions, however, the research might be conducted by a related department, such as marketing or personnel. At American Family Insurance Group, a midwestern insurance firm headquartered in Madison, Wisconsin, employee attitude surveys are regularly administered under the direction of the personnel department. The results are made available to the employees through a variety of channels, including the employee newsletter, published by the PR department.

Although much of this research is conducted in-house, a large portion is conducted by outside research consultants. These consultants have a specialized research expertise that PR practitioners often lack. External consultants also offer an independent, objective point of view that someone inside an organization might lack.

Yet another source of PR research comes from public opinion firms. Polling organizations such as Gallup or Roper Polls frequently conduct opinion research on issues related to public relations. Examples include presidential popularity polls or surveys on the credibility of public institutions, such as business or government.

WHY STUDY PUBLIC RELATIONS?

Social scientists have generally agreed that there are several specific purposes for conducting research: (1) to describe, (2) to explain, and (3) to predict. *Descriptive research* is designed to paint a picture of a process, situation, or phenomenon. It tells us what is happening or what something's or someone's characteristics are. *Explanatory research* tells us why something happens. It tells us what the causes and effects are. *Predictive research* tells us what will or probably will happen if we do or do not do something. Each of these types of research helps increase our understanding of people, society, and the world.

All of these are reasons for studying public relations. We want research to tell us about the process of public relations, to tell us what will and will not work. We conduct research to explain how public relations works—what forces can influence public opinion or behavior.

PR research gives us a glimpse of society itself. Public relations, like advertising, is one of the principal support industries for the mass media. PR people provide much of the information and content of the news. Public relations also serves as a vital link between many important individuals and institutions and the public.

Because of this significant role, many scholars are motivated to understand the exact nature, effect, and function of public relations in our society and the world. They also seek to understand the standards and ethics of those who practice public relations. For many, the ultimate goal is to legitimize the practice of public relations by making it a full-fledged profession, like law or medicine.

1

THE NATURE OF THE BEAST

Systematic research is playing an increasingly important role in public relations, as practitioners seek greater acceptance by management and academicians explore the process and effects of the field.

Counselors of public relations deal in intangibles, the art of persuasion. As television journalist Bill Moyers (1983) said in *The Imagemakers*, PR counselors often use "the alchemy" of publicity to turn tarnished images into gold—or at least give them a golden lining. How can one measure such a process? What can research tell us? That is the subject of this book.

Research is the systematic collection and interpretation of information. Its basic purpose is to increase understanding. Research can be used to answer a variety of questions, from determining the gravitational pull of the earth to predicting the next appearance of Halley's Comet. When applied to the study of human behavior, research is used to answer questions about the effects of television violence on viewer aggression, or a PR campaign on public attitudes toward some corporation.

Notably, when we use the term *research*, we are not referring to all forms of study, such as library research. Instead, we are talking about empirical studies involving the systematic collection and interpretation of data, such as Gallup public opinion polls.

Systematic research often takes the form of social science methods, such as public opinion surveys, laboratory experiments, or "IQ" tests. Until the late 1970s, few attempts were made to apply these or any systematic methods to the study of public relations. A study by Grunig and Hickson (1976) reveals that of 4,141 articles or books on public relations published prior to 1976, only 63 dealt with research. The remainder—more than 98%—were not systematic or scholarly, but descriptive and anecdotal in nature.

In preparing this book, the author and a Pennsylvania State University journalism graduate student, Ann Summerall, undertook a systematic analysis of all PR research published since 1975 in six leading communication research journals and PR trade publications. These publications include the scholarly journals *Journalism Quarterly*, *Public Opinion Quarterly*, *Public Relations Review*, and *Public Relations Research and Education* and the PR industry trade journals, *Public Relations Journal* and *Public Relations Quarterly*.

Our census of the years 1975 to 1985 reveals that 34% of all 2,000 articles published in these journals deal specifically with PR research issues. This is clearly a significant increase in the volume of PR research in recent years. More specifically, this review shows that there was an average of 18 systematic research studies on public relations published each year from 1975 to 1979. This number has increased to almost 28 such articles a year since then. In 1985 there were more than 40 systematic PR studies published in the journals reviewed.

As the Commission on Public Relations Education reported in 1975, "Basic, original research by PR educators and PR practitioners is noted more for its absence than its existence." *Basic research* is a special type of research that is especially lacking in the field of public relations. It is research designed to build theory—not to answer specific practical problems.

The Pavlik-Summerall content analysis shows that only a fraction of the past 10 years of PR research has been basic research. Most has dealt with specific, practical problems or issues. It has not been the kind designed to build a general, theoretical body of knowledge about public relations. This, of course, is fundamental for public relations to become a "true" profession.

The commission explains, "Most PR educators—not having attained the Ph.D. level—have not been required to do such research, have not learned how to do it, or have not been interested in doing it. Most of them, indeed, are teaching skills courses that have little relationship to basic research."

Other communication scholars often have viewed public relations as a second-class discipline—if that—and unworthy of their attention. Most have preferred to study the more "respectable" field of journalism. In fact, the first scholarly journal on PR research, *Public Relations Review*, was founded just 12 years ago. In comparison, *Journalism Quarterly* was founded more than 60 years ago, in 1924. It is also just one of numerous journals devoted to the scholarly study of journalism. This is also reflected in the negative manner in which most mass communication texts portray PR professionals as "journalists who sold out" (Cline, 1982).

Even fewer PR practitioners have attempted any systematic research—basic or applied. For most of the twentieth century, PR people had come from the field of journalism, in particular, newspapers. Ivy Ledbetter Lee, perhaps the first modern PR practitioner, had been a newspaper man for most of his professional career. In 1914, he left journalism to do PR work for John D. Rockefeller, Sr. Lee was called in to shape up Rockefeller's tarnished public image. His tool: publicity. Most PR people who followed Lee also came from a journalism background. Trained in communication, they knew little about systematic research.

Many also felt they did not need to use research. As Dr. Willard L. Thompson, of the University of Minnesota points out (1986), "I'll libel the PR people, but too many of them assume they have some special insight into publics, and how to control them." They often don't have any special insight, as an exploratory survey by Larry Judd (1986) reveals. His findings indicate that practitioners are not especially perceptive of public opinion or attitudes about current issues or events. Rather, practitioners need research "to verify hunches about public attitudes before they begin expensive or crucial campaigns." Pioneer PR man Edward L. Bernays adds his clear viewpoint, "Time has shown us that you are stupid to assume anything about the public."

Not until the mid-1970s did things begin to change for the field of public relations. A sagging economy began to put new pressure on PR practitioners to document their importance in the corporate world. Marketing and advertising personnel could demonstrate their value in terms of dollars and cents. PR professionals needed to find evidence of their value—research helped provide the evidence (Finn, 1982).

Although public relations is vital to organizational existence—this is particularly evident in crisis situations, such as cases of product tampering in which public relations plays a critical role in the dissemination of information to the public—its value is rarely documented. This has made public relations especially vulnerable during tight economic times. A recent example of this vulnerability is provided by the 1986 CBS firings—over 500 persons were fired, a great many of whom filled PR-related positions.

"The crunch is on," explains Gerald Wollan, a senior counselor at Padilla & Speer, a leading Minneapolis-based PR agency. "Profits must be maintained, and PR must document its importance to management. Research is one way to do this." Practitioner Lloyd Kirban (1983) adds, "Showing what we do makes a difference . . . it is important if PR is to be accepted by management." "The 20th Century has seen the development of management science in business," reports John Beardsley, Chief Executive Officer of Padilla & Speer. Beardsley explains that public relations has only recently begun to participate in this trend by learning the science of communication. "Research is vital to this process," he adds. "It helps take the guess work out of PR. . . . It also helps establish PR as a management function."

As PR practitioners have developed the research function, they have also begun to enjoy greater status in corporate America. A survey of Fortune 500 (Skinner & Shanklin, 1978) companies found that as the PR function in large business organizations has grown more important and complex, practitioners have gained stature in the hierarchy. They are receiving increased budgetary support, more access to top management, and more influence on corporate decision making and planning.

The nature of the PR practitioner also has been evolving. Women are entering the field in large numbers, often bringing with them a new perspective. They also have begun to emerge as leaders of the field. Since 1980, the Public Relations Society of America (PRSA) has twice been headed by women, Judith S. Bogart in 1983 and Barbara W. Hunter in 1984.

Entrants to the field are also no longer exclusively trained in journalism or media studies. Many come from a variety of backgrounds, including sociology, psychology, and marketing. The most successful were trained not only in communication but the psychology of human behavior. These new practitioners are not the first to apply psychological principles to public relations. As early as 1923, Bernays, a nephew of Sigmund Freud, laid the groundwork for a social-scientific approach to public relations in his book, *Crystallizing Public Opinion*—the first ever on public relations. His book also signals a long-standing connection between PR and public opinion research, a research tradition dating to the 1920s.

PR historian Marvin Olasky (1984) reports that Bernays was a "seminal thinker concerning the means of synthesizing the new, Freudian perspective on man with the older practices of the publicist's trade." Further, the principles "Bernays developed and expounded were radical in both origin and application."

Bernays's contribution to the social scientific approach goes even beyond public relations, as a letter from the master surveyor Paul Lazarsfeld reveals. Lazarsfeld, who at one time lived in Bernays's home, was a leading figure in studies of media effects. In a personal letter, Lazarsfeld revealed that Bernays helped him develop some of his basic views of media processes and effects.

As is reflected in Bernays's activities and Lazarsfeld's letter, the origins of PR research actually date to the 1920s—predating the earliest research in the print and broadcast media. Ironically, these fields today have well-developed research traditions, while public relations does not. For example, the broadcast media since the 1930s have been accumulating research-based knowledge about their audiences and programs. Meanwhile, research is only today emerging as an integral part of the "scientific method" of public relations—as the new practitioners help Bernays's ideas diffuse throughout the profession.

Paralleling the development of the field of public relations was the development of the advertising industry. In the early 1900s, it too was a rather unscientific field, with outrageous ads claiming everything from hair restoration to miracle cures. With the growth of the mass media, especially television, this once-simple field evolved into a complex, sophisticated industry with research at the core of the machinery. Modern advertising leaves little to chance. Target audiences are identified and studied; commercials are pretested and posttested; entire campaigns are researched in test market situations.

The field of public relations has not been so systematic. As community relations expert Louis Graff (1981) laments, "There simply has not been enough meaningful, controlled research in public relations and communications to assure people that we really know what we are doing when advising them to pursue a certain program.... We have not been . . . scholarly in our approach to our profession."

Why has public relations lagged so far behind advertising in its use of research? Perhaps part of the reason is due to a difference in scope—U.S. corporations annually spend tens of billions of dollars on advertising, and only a fraction of this on public relations.

Perhaps research has played a greater role in advertising because advertising is pointed directly at the bottom line—sales—and its impact is readily apparent.

However, there may be a more important reason. PR campaigns, unlike their advertising counterparts, have been plagued by vague, ambiguous objectives. Changing the company's image and improving media relations are examples of typically vague objectives. Sometimes, objectives simply may not exist, or if they do, they are stated in terms of activities—how many press releases will be issued—rather than outcomes—the desired effect. How can research be conducted without first knowing what is to be accomplished?

Public relations also has tended to be a reactive discipline. Since the time of Ivy Lee, PR practitioners have spent much of their time "putting out fires," rather than developing systematic plans to prevent them. Consider Lee's first assignment for Rockefeller. Miners working for

Rockefeller in southern Colorado went on strike in 1914, seeking better working conditions and a livable wage. Rockefeller responded by sending in the militia. The result: the Ludlow Massacre—53 civilians dead, including 16 women and children. Public opinion immediately sided with the miners, and Lee was called in to do something—fast. There was scant time for systematic research and no available source of research either.

It seemed that little had changed when the Commission on Public Relations Education (1975) offered this commentary, "PR practitioners ... generally have been too busy at their jobs to engage in basic research, not connected with specific PR tasks." Debra Kelley Vaughn, public relations practitioner for the Saint Paul (Minnesota) Children's Hospital elaborates (1982), "Public relations departments are generally under-staffed and underbudgeted, forcing them to allocate most of their time and money to producing public relations products and services, and little to research." With an increased budget, PR practitioners might find more room for research.

Vaughn further explains that PR departments are often under great day-to-day pressure to produce news releases, provide counseling for other members of the organization who are not experienced in PR techniques, and react to a variety of unforeseen crises.

Thus, for many reasons PR research has been slow to develop. Neither academics nor practitioners have had the background, interests, or resources to conduct substantial basic research. The commission concluded its report by stating that at least three conditions must be met before we will see any real improvement:

(1) Educators must take an increased interest in doing basic research;
(2) those in PR education must define the areas that constitute "basic" research in public relations; and
(3) PR organizations and practitioners must develop a willingness to supply the funds for more research activities.

In recent years, public relations educators and practitioners have begun to grapple seriously with these issues. In 1984 the first issue of *Public Relations Research and Education*, a journal "devoted to scholarly research and teaching of public relations," appeared. Founding editor James E. Grunig has encouraged authors to submit basic, theory-building research. Unfortunately, as Grunig (1986) recently admitted, "There are still too few people conducting basic research in public relations."

The International Association of Business Communicators (IABC) recently funded a major basic research investigation to be undertaken by an academic research team headed by Grunig. Now in the planning stages, this five-year study may set the agenda for future PR research. Its focus is on identifying what communication contributes to the goals of an organization.

Figure 1.1 presents a historical overview of the milestones in the brief history of PR research. These include Herbert Hyman and Paul Sheatley's (1947) government-sponsored study that reveals the importance of the psychological barriers to communication, Bernays's (1955) conceptualization of a systematic approach to public relations and the role of research, Grunig's (1976) situational view of the public, and the IABC study (current) to determine the contribution of public relations to organizational effectiveness.

A growing number of universities are now offering advanced degrees in public relations. The University of Georgia, the University of Maryland, and Rutgers each offers a doctoral degree in public relations. Students graduating from these programs will have both the training and interest to conduct basic research in public relations.

Simply increasing the production of basic research about public relations, however, will not be satisfactory. Roy J. Leffingwell (1980) explains in a regular *Public Relations Journal* column focusing on the practitioner-social scientist communication gap:

> Hundreds of articles are published on group behavior and social services delivery—only to be read by other scholars. The scholars argue that practitioners should be more sophisticated in applying the results of current research. The practitioners complain that the research is garbled by technical jargon and is often irrelevant to the real world.

Leffingwell (1981-1982) adds, "Social science research findings could save us a great deal of money."

PR research will fully realize its potential only when this "communication gap" has been overcome.

THEMES OF THE RESEARCH

Most research on public relations is either applied or basic (see Figure 1.2). *Applied research* is designed to solve practical problems. *Basic research* is designed to build theory about the PR process. As Grunig (1979b) suggests, the most valuable basic research is applied to or tested using specific practical problems. A third major research theme

1923--Bernays' Crystallizing Public Opinion published--lays
      foundation for systematic approach to public relations.
1937--Public Opinion Quarterly publishes first issue, with
      Bernays' report on trends in PR activities.
1947--Hyman and Sheatsley's "Some Reasons Why Information Campaigns
      Fail"--outlines psychological barriers to communication.
1955--Bernays' Engineering of Consent published--elaborates
      systematic approach to PR and role of research.
1972--McGuire's "Attitude change: The information-processing
      paradigm" summarizes research to date on classic persuasion
      process.
1976--Grunig's "Communication Behaviors Occurring in Decision
      and Non-Decision Situations" introduces principles of
      a situational view of persuasion in PR.
1977--Lerbinger's "Corporate Uses of Research" provides framework
      for understanding the function of PR research.
1979--Broom and Smith's "Testing Practitioner's Impact on Clients"
      explores roles in PR.
1984--Grunig's "Organizations, Environments and Models of Public
      Relations" develops structural view of PR.
1986--IABC study by Grunig and others to determine the contribution
      of PR to organizational effectiveness- five-year investigation
      is largest PR study to date.

Figure 1.1 Milestones in the History of PR Research

encompasses what we call *introspective research. Introspective research*
represents studies that look inwardly at the profession itself.

SOLVING PROBLEMS

Applied research is directed at specific practical issues. It involves
two main research subthemes: strategic and evaluation.

Strategic research is used primarily in campaign or program development. It is situational and problem oriented. An organization will most
often use this kind of research in the planning process. Studies can be
used to help determine objectives and establish a baseline. They can also
be used to identify or stay in touch with various publics, and to develop
message or media strategy. Much of this research is devoted to the
examination of the tools and techniques of public relations.

Evaluation research is conducted primarily to determine the effectiveness of a PR program. Effectiveness is defined in terms of the
accomplishment of various goals and objectives. Some evaluation
research simply asks whether the goals and objectives were met. This is
called *summative research*. It represents the bottom line. A second kind
of evaluation research is called *formative research*. It serves as a tool for
improving the effectiveness of future PR efforts. Formative research is
usually conducted before a campaign, although it may continue
throughout the campaign as a way to monitor its progress and keep it
running most effectively and efficiently.

Themes	Applied Research	Basic Research	Introspective Research
Examples	**Strategic** Research confirms the growing importance of corporate advertising in PR strategy (Patti and McDonald, 1984)	Recent investigations challenge long-held notions of attitude and behavior change: a new situational view emerges (Grunig, 1984)	Survey research shows significant differences between the salaries and roles of male and female practitioners: males are paid more and are more likely to occupy manager roles (Broom, 1982)
	Evaluation Studies show three evaluation styles: Informal seat of the pants; scientific impact; scientific dissemination (Dozier, 1985)		

Figure 1.2   Research Themes in Public Relations

BUILDING THEORY

Basic research, in general, is not designed to solve any particular problem. Instead, it can be applied across situations and is designed to build a "basic" body of knowledge upon which future research or problem solving can rest.

Devoted to theory building, *basic research* is abstract and conceptual, and intended to increase understanding, explain cause-and-effect relationships, and predict future situations or conditions. Its focus is on the processes underlying the PR field. For example, much basic research has been designed to improve our understanding of the nature of the public(s), organizations, and public opinion.

LOOKING INWARD

Introspective research encompasses a broad range of investigations that focus on the PR function itself and the higher educational system that supports that function. This research represents a form of self-examination. Research questions include: Is public relations truly a profession? What are the standards and practices of public relations? What are the characteristics of practitioners? What are the nature and function of professional associations in public relations? And, do the undergraduate and graduate PR curricula in American universities adequately prepare future generations of PR practitioners, educators, and researchers?

It is important to note that some research may fall into more than one research theme. For example, research on PR roles is primarily introspective, but it does aid our basic, theoretical understanding of the nature of the field. Thus, the reader should treat these themes as ideal types, or categories for organizing our research-based knowledge about public relations.

The basis for these themes lies in the motivations of the scholars studying public relations. The following section examines these motivations.

MOTIVATIONS FOR DOING RESEARCH ON PUBLIC RELATIONS

Advancing the Profession

Scholars studying public relations have many motivations for doing so. In the academic world, some seek to better understand public relations as a form of communication, some to advance the profession, and some simply to publish articles in order to get tenure at a university. According to Grunig (1983b), "The role of public relations educators and academic researchers should be to serve the profession: to conduct research that will advance the profession and train the next generation of practitioners." This is clearly the strongest motivation for studying public relations among those in the academic community. Educators in this area tend to identify strongly with the profession. They have often worked in the field and maintain an association with the industry. Many are members of PR associations. They also often serve as advisors to students who hope to work in the PR field.

All told, PR educators are motivated to enhance the profession that they are educating students to enter. They are also motivated to monitor the profession. They seek to understand the changing nature of the practice and methods of public relations, the practitioners, and the standards and ethics of the field. For many, the primary goal is to study these things to build a body of knowledge upon which the practice of public relations can rest. Only in this way can public relations achieve the full professional status many hope for.

At the same time, many PR educators who conduct research hold Ph.D. degrees, generally in communication or other social science fields. In the social sciences, a Ph.D. is generally a research and teaching degree. As such, persons holding Ph.D.'s tend to have a scholarly outlook on the world. This means they look at things in an abstract, often theoretical way. They look for patterns and tendencies.

Those in the social sciences are first interested in understanding human behavior. Those who study public relations are interested in it as a form of human behavior—this goes beyond the study of public relations in isolation. It means taking a broader view of public relations, an interdisciplinary view. This motivation has led many researchers to apply theoretical ideas from other fields to the study of public relations. It also motivates some to develop ideas about public relations that go beyond public relations.

Since public relations has traditionally been viewed as a form of persuasive communication, many scholars have been motivated to study it as such. They have studied the PR communication process to see how general communication principles apply. They have also sought to integrate the specifics of public relations into the general discipline of communication. Finally, many academic researchers are motivated to improve our understanding of the field of public relations and its role in society. A growing body of original research is designed to build a theory or theories of the process and effects of public relations. In the corporate world, probably the most fundamental motivation to do PR research is to solve problems in the field. These problems are clearly reflected in the corporate uses of PR research.

ORGANIZATIONAL USES OF RESEARCH

It's been almost a decade since his landmark study, but no one has yet provided a more definitive summary of the corporate uses of PR research than Professor and PR consultant Otto Lerbinger. In 1977, Lerbinger reported the results of a Foundation for Public Relations Research and Education survey of 28 major corporations and nonprofit organizations. The organizations include Roper Public Opinion Research Center, Inc., a center that has surveys dating to the 1930s; Louis Harris and Associates' Survey; and Yankelovich, Skelly and White's Corporate Priorities Survey. While this sampling plan does not represent all organizations using PR research, it is nevertheless useful as an exploratory study.

The foundation's survey, as reported by Lerbinger, indicates that there are four basic types or uses of PR research in the corporate and nonprofit worlds (see Figure 1.3): (1) environmental monitoring, (2) public relations audits, (3) communications audits, and (4) social audits. This categorization is especially significant, since prior to Lerbinger's

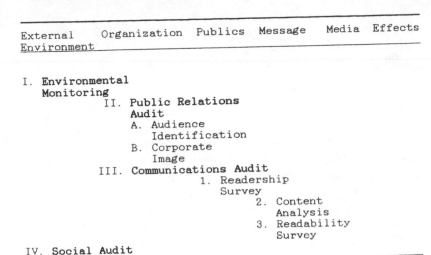

External Environment	Organization	Publics	Message	Media	Effects

I. Environmental
   Monitoring
               II. Public Relations
                   Audit
                   A. Audience
                      Identification
                   B. Corporate
                      Image
           III. Communications Audit
                           1. Readership
                              Survey
                                   2. Content
                                      Analysis
                                   3. Readability
                                      Survey
IV. Social Audit

Figure 1.3 Corporate Uses of Research (after Lerbinger, 1977)

study, PR research had been defined by method rather than by function. For example, when talking about research, PR practitioners would often mention various techniques, such as content analysis or readability studies. But, they rarely examined the greater question of how that research was used.

Figure 1.3 presents Lerbinger's four uses of research, each listed under the appropriate heading: the external environment, organization, publics, message, media, and effects.

Environmental Monitoring

Listed under the headings of both the external environment and the organization, *environmental monitoring* encompasses what Lerbinger considers the mainstay of PR research: studies of public opinion. In the world of business, this is often referred to as *assessing the corporate climate*. Most corporations recognize that they are part of a social system, and that changes in the environment may have significant effects on their welfare. Thus, there is a great need to monitor continually "trends in public opinion and events in the sociopolitical environment."

This need was well articulated by one respondent in the study, Frank T. LeBart of John Hancock Mutual Life Insurance Company's advertising and PR department: "We consider it important that this department and John Hancock in general be kept well informed on trends in political thinking, changes in social values as well as perceived social needs. We feel that John Hancock must be aware of the 'changing environment' in which we must operate." Environmental monitoring, LeBart points out, offers the opportunity to identify and prevent problems—"before they have reached a magnitude and momentum as to permit only hasty improvised reaction."

Opinion researcher Tom W. Smith (1980) provides a useful example of environmental monitoring based on 30 years of Gallup poll data, from 1946 to 1976 . He conducted a trend analysis of 200 surveys conducted by Gallup since World War II in order to identify America's most important problem. He found that the most important problem, as identified by those polled, is tied to historical events, and varies by sociodemographic group.

During the first 20 years (1946-1966), when there was much concern about a cold war, foreign affairs often headed the list. Since 1966, foreign affairs has fallen off in importance, but civil rights has seen a rise in importance.

Public Relations Audit

Although environmental monitoring is the mainstay of PR research, the PR audit is the most widely used research category. The PR audit is designed to evaluate an organization's standing with its relevant publics. Thus, it is listed under both the organization and the publics.

According to Lerbinger's survey, there are two basic types of PR audits—audience identification and corporate image studies. The former has four basic steps. First, the researcher must identify all relevant publics. A public is considered relevant on the following basis: Does our organization (or may it in the future) have some effect on the public, or does this public (or may it in the future) have some effect on our organization?

Second, the researcher must evaluate the organization's standing with each relevant public. Here the focus is on public perceptions, attitudes, and involvement with the organization.

Third, the researcher must identify issues of concern to those publics.

And, finally, he or she must measure the power of each public. What is the extent of its resources, including financial, human, and other.

A corporate image study is almost an extension of step two of the PR audit. Here the researcher determines: (1) the familiarity of each public with the organization, (2) the attitudes of each public toward the organization, and (3) the personality characteristics each public associates with the organization.

For instance, a PR researcher for AT&T might conduct a corporate image study to determine the extent to which AT&T customers understand the company's recent divestiture. How has this change affected customer attitudes toward AT&T? Do customers see AT&T as a cold, impersonal corporation, or do they associate more positive personality characteristics with the new AT&T.

Wollan (1986) of Padilla & Speer suggests four situations when his agency uses the PR audit (although they call it a *communication audit* to increase its marketability, especially to governmental agencies). "We use research when we are working with a new client, when the client has a change of direction (such as a name change), when there is new management, or when management senses a problem."

Communications Audit

PR practitioners spend much of their time engaged in communications activities. It is only right that one of the most important corporate uses of research involves assessing those communication activities. Thus, the third use identified in Lerbinger's survey is the *communications audit*, a use that applies to every heading, except the external environment.

The communications audit has been widely used to study the readability and readership of corporate newsletters, and to a lesser extent other routine communications, such as annual reports and press releases.

Practitioner James B. Strenski (1982) notes, "A communication audit undertaken a year after the communications program has been modified, based on the first audit effort, will help keep the communications program on track, communicating with its publics cost effectively."

Social Audit

The final corporate use of research is known as the *social audit*. Its primary purpose is to examine the organization's performance as corporate citizen. How does the corporation stack up in the community? Are its manufacturing procedures conducive to a healthy environment? Is the organization more than a system of inputs and outputs designed for the sole purpose of making maximum profit? All these motivations have led to a rapidly growing body of research on public relations. In the next section, we will discuss the research methods that have been used to study public relations.

SUMMARY

It is clear that as the field of public relations has grown over the past half century, so has the need for research. The production of both basic and applied research has not met this need, for a variety of reasons. PR practitioners have had neither the time nor the resources, and PR educators have lacked the prerequisite graduate training and interest to conduct scholarly research. Topping this off, the tarnished image of public relations has kept many scholars in academic circles outside public relations from conducting research in this area.

As more universities recognize the significance of the PR field, and as "management by objectives" becomes a growing force in PR practice, we will continue to see an increase in the production of PR research.

2

MAJOR RESEARCH METHODS

Researchers studying public relations have used tools from the social sciences, especially mail and telephone surveys.

The term *research method* means many things. It can refer to how data are collected, how a study is designed, or how the data are analyzed. Most fundamentally, it refers to how knowledge is obtained.

Sociologists David and Chava Nachmias (1976) say that there are at least four "methods" of obtaining knowledge: the authoritarian method, the mystical method, the rationalistic method, and the scientific method. In the authoritarian method, knowledge is generated by persons socially or politically identified as "qualified producers of knowledge." These might be oracles in a tribal society, kings in a monarchical society, or scientists in a technocratic society. Knowledge in the mystical method is produced by prophets, mediums, or other persons deriving their power from the supernatural. The rationalistic method generates knowledge through a process of explanation. Explanations are based on formal logic. The following syllogism illustrates this process:

All A are B.

All B are C.

Therefore all A are C.

In the scientific method, knowledge is generated through systematic observations of our world. It is based on the premise that knowledge is "a product of one's experiences as facets of the physical, biological and social world play upon the senses" (Sjoberg & Nett, 1968).

Systematic research on public relations deals primarily with knowledge generated through the scientific method. It is based upon systematic observations of PR phenomena. Scholars call this *empirical research*. One must be careful when interpreting such knowledge, however. Not everything is measurable, quantifiable. Further, numbers have a way of taking on added or inflated importance and definitiveness.

Wollan (1986) of Padilla & Speer adds his concern about a preoccupation with quantitative measurement: "We must be careful not to count things that are superficial." Thus, the communication audit at Padilla & Speer makes heavy use of subjective, qualitative analyses, as well as quantitative ones. This approach helps answer the *why* as well as the *what*.

Many qualitative methods are quite systematic and quite valuable sources of intelligence about public relations. They simply do not make heavy use of quantitative, statistical methods of data collection and interpretation. Some of these methods, such as historical or legal research, are very well known. Since these methods are not empirically based, however, we will not focus on findings from this research.

Nevertheless, quantitative research provides valuable knowledge about public relations. Alan K. Leahigh, Senior Vice President, Public Communications, Inc., puts it this way (1985-1986): "If you can't count it, does it count? Perhaps, but counting it is the only way to be sure."

In making systematic observations, researchers studying public relations employ three basic data collection methods. The methods are (1) survey research, (2) unobtrusive measures (e.g., content analysis), and (3) observational methods (e.g., experiments). Survey research and unobtrusive measures are the most prevalent. Observational methods, although quite powerful, are typically more expensive and require a greater commitment of time and human resources.

These methods come from the social sciences. They have been used and tested extensively in many well-established fields, including sociology, economics, and marketing. Scholars use them to study public relations for several reasons. First, public relations lends itself naturally to examination by these methods. Social science research methods are designed to study human behavior, especially that involving groups and organizations. Bernays calls public relations an "applied social science." A second reason for employing social science research methods in the study of public relations has to do with the background and training of those who do the research. Most of the researchers come from a social science background. Their education is in sociology, psychology, or communication. Since they have studied the research methods of the social sciences, it is only logical that they would use these methods to conduct their own research.

SURVEY RESEARCH

Survey research is the most frequently used research method in public relations. Surveys are used to do everything from monitor public opinion to assess employee attitudes. Pavlik and Summerall's (1986) content analysis of the leading PR publication outlets shows that about two-thirds (67%) of the published studies over the past 10 years used the survey method. PR research in the private, corporate sector also makes heavy use of survey research. As Gary Schmermund, Director of PR research at AT&T corporate headquarters in New York, reports (1986), "The bulk of our research has probably employed survey sampling. We use it in all areas, from employee communications to public policy research."

Survey research comes in two basic packages: descriptive and analytical. *Descriptive surveys* are ones that develop a picture of a current situation or condition. They tell us how many employees are satisfied with their job, or what percentage of the consumer public recognizes our new corporate logo. They are also usually taken at one point in time, much like a photograph. Thus, descriptive surveys cannot offer much in the way of explaining cause-and-effect relationships. They cannot tell us how "effective" a PR program has been.

Descriptive surveys are usually cross-sectional in nature. This means they are taken at one point in time. They provide a "cross-sectional" view of the population under study. Taking a cross-sectional survey is similar to eating a slice of pie. We get a taste of each part of the pie—the crust, the filling—but we don't know how the pie came to be—what the ingredients are, at what temperature it was baked or for how long. In a cross-sectional survey, we get a glimpse of the different segments of the population, but we don't know how they came to be.

Analytical surveys are designed to answer the questions that descriptive surveys cannot. Their purpose is to help describe and explain why a current situation or condition exists. For example, an analytical survey might address the question of why employees read company newsletters, or why a community relations program failed to achieve its objectives. Analytical surveys usually involve the statistical testing of research hypotheses. While analytical surveys can be cross-sectional, they are often taken at more than one moment in time. This allows the researcher to study cause-and-effect relationships. In public relations, for example, a researcher might survey employee attitudes immediately before implementing a new internal relations program, and shortly after instituting the program. Any changes in employee attitudes could be attributed to the new program. A survey is simply a list of questions designed to elicit information from a set of individuals. Whether descriptive or analytical, there are two basic issues involved in conducting a survey: (1) developing the list of questions and (2) determining the set of individuals.

Measurement

The first issue involves what researchers call *measurement*. Measurement is the process of assigning numbers to the object of study. We do this in everyday life when we measure a distance with a yardstick. In survey research, we do this when we "measure" someone's opinion. For example, in an employee attitude survey a researcher might ask employees to rate the company's benefits program, using a 1- to 10-point scale—where one means poor, and ten means excellent.

The primary concern is whether the measurement is "valid" and "reliable." By *valid* we mean, "Does the measurement instrument—the questionnaire—actually measure what it is supposed to?" In our everyday example, a yardstick is valid if it is actually 36 inches in length. In the employee attitude survey, our concern would be whether the question actually measures the employee's feelings about the company's benefits program. If an employee has no basis for comparison, what meaning does his or her answer have? *Reliability* refers to the consistency of the measure. A yardstick is a reliable measure if it produces the same results on each use. Similarly, an item on an employee attitude survey is reliable if it produces the same results on each use.

Surveys can come in a variety of forms. There are structured versus unstructured questionnaires, open-ended versus closed-ended questions, disguised versus undisguised questions. PR research most often involves the use of structured questionnaires, and a mix of open- and closed-ended undisguised questions. They can also be administered in a variety of ways. Surveys can be taken over the telephone, by mail, or face to face. In public relations, the most common technique is the mail questionnaire (67%), with about an equal mix of phone (17%) and face-to-face (15%) interviews.

This represents a major methodological issue in the field of PR research. Mail questionnaire administration is used for several reasons, especially its low cost. Unfortunately, mail questionnaires have several serious flaws that jeopardize their validity and reliability. For example, mail questionnaires usually get low response rates—between 30% and 50% of the people surveyed return usable questionnaires. One also cannot be sure who filled out the questionnaire. In medicine, doctors sometimes have a nurse fill out mail questionnaires because they are too busy to do it themselves. A similar problem may occur in surveys of executives, with secretaries filling out a questionnaire intended for a CEO. Furthermore, mail questionnaires are generally unable to elicit the same kind or level of information that a face-to-face or even a telephone survey might obtain. Therefore, PR research must move away from its heavy reliance on mail questionnaires and begin greater use of face-to-face or telephone interviewing.

Each approach has certain advantages and disadvantages. Some are more expensive, some are able to obtain different kinds of information. The fundamental issue, however, remains: Does the survey validly and reliably measure the information it is designed to obtain?

Sampling

The second basic issue in survey research involves determining the set of individuals to collect information from. There are two basic approaches to this problem. They are drawing a *sample* and taking a *census*. In both approaches one begins by defining the population. The *population* is what PR practitioners refer to as a *public*, such as employees, shareholders, or consumers.

The two approaches differ at this point. In a *census*, one surveys everyone in the population. This process is very expensive and time consuming. But, it does have several advantages, especially when the public is fairly small. It means information is collected from all members of the public—and this is often important from a PR point of view. For example, employee attitude surveys are generally based on a census, in order to convince each employee that management is interested in what he or she has to say.

Sampling involves selecting a subset of the population and making generalizations from that sample to the broader population. Drawing a sample is less expensive than taking a census, and if done properly, can give information as accurately as a census (some even say more accurately than a census!).

The logic behind survey sampling is much the same as in taking a blood sample. One need not drain all the blood from a patient to determine his or her blood type. The same is true in survey research. One need not interview all members of a population to determine the prevailing opinion on some issue facing that population. The key is to obtain a truly representative sample.

Two approaches are used in obtaining a sample: probability sampling and nonprobability sampling. *Probability sampling* is what one might commonly view as the "scientific" method, while *nonprobability sampling* is a more informal approach. The real power of probability sampling is that it enables the researcher to make statistical inferences from the sample to the broader population.

Nonprobability samples come in two basic forms. First, there is what's called a *convenience sample*. A *convenience sample* is one in which survey subjects are selected on a "whoever-happens-to-be-there" basis. They aren't very systematic, but they are inexpensive. Journalists often use convenience samples when they conduct "man-on-the-street" polls. These samples do not produce "scientifically valid" results, but they do provide a glimpse of what some viewpoints are on certain issues.

In public relations, convenience samples might be used in focus group interviews. A *focus group interview* is a relatively unstructured surveying technique in which a moderator asks two or more people questions about a certain topic. The subjects are allowed to answer in whatever form they wish, while the moderator's job is to keep the "focus" of the discussion on the topic at hand. Focus groups are useful for generating ideas and are especially useful during the early stages of campaign planning. The results are often used to help formulate more specific research hypotheses for subsequent testing. Advertisers often conduct focus group interviews at shopping malls, where subjects are easily recruited. PR counsel F. Michael Lorz (1984) used focus group research to help target messages and identify "persuadable" publics in an election campaign.

Academics often use a type of convenience sample known as *available sampling*. In this method, a professor might use students in his or her class as subjects. This method is very inexpensive, but is criticized on the basis of having little "external validity." That is, findings from a student-based sample may not be generalized to the rest of the population.

The second type of nonprobability sample is called a *purposive sample*. Here, the researcher is looking for a person with certain characteristics. He or she selects as many subjects as needed, on the basis of whether they have those characteristics. A similar method is known as *quota sampling*. In a quota sample, a researcher is looking for a specific number of people who have certain characteristics. For example, a researcher for the Board of Trustees at a U.S. university might be investigating public opinion on the South Africa divestment issue. He or she might wish to interview 200 people, 100 students and 100 faculty members. Rather than randomly selecting 200 persons, and hoping for a 50-50 split, the researcher might systematically select 100 persons from each group. Again, this method is not "scientifically valid," but it is less expensive than a probability sample.

Probability sampling is a technique in which all members of a population have a "known chance of being selected." This is a mathematical criterion that allows researchers to use various statistical tests to make generalizations from the sample to the total population. There are four types of probability samples: simple random sampling, systematic sampling, stratified sampling, and cluster sampling.

A *simple random sample* is the basic probability sampling method. It is also the most difficult and expensive. It requires that all members of the population have an equal nonzero chance of being selected. To draw a simple random sample, one must first identify all members of the population. Then, one "randomly" selects as many subjects as needed from that list, one subject at a time. Computers are normally used as an aid in making the random selections. The hardest part in this process is developing the list of the population.

Systematic sampling is closely related to simple random sampling, but is somewhat easier and less expensive. One begins by developing a list of the population. Rather than selecting each person randomly, however, one selects only a random starting point in the list. From then on, the researcher selects every Nth person in the list. To illustrate, suppose a researcher desires a sample of 100 and has a population of 10,000. In a systematic sample, he merely selects a random starting point from the first 100 persons and then picks every hundredth person thereafter (i.e., $10,000/100 = N$). Technically, the systematic sample is not a perfect probability sampling plan—not everyone has an equal probability of being selected since inclusion is based on the random starting point.

A stratified sample is used when the researcher wants to be sure to include persons from different segments (i.e., strata) of the population. In public relations, a researcher might use a stratified sampling plan if he or she wishes to include persons from several distinct publics. While this method is much less expensive than simple random or systematic sampling, it does require some prior knowledge of the population. Specifically, the researcher must know the size and nature of the population strata to be sampled. For example, consider the situation at a large corporation that employs more than 30,000 workers worldwide. We want to see if there is a relationship between number of years with the company and readership of the company newsletter. Let's say we know that 50% of our employees have been with the company more than five years, 40% one to five years, and 10% less than a year. A simple random sample of 100 persons might not give us exactly 50 employees with more than five years' experience, 40 with one to five years' experience, and 10 with less than one years' experience. Using a stratified technique, however, we could be sure to obtain exactly the right number from each group.

Simple random, systematic, and stratified samples are often prohibitively expensive when large-scale studies are being conducted. Instead, researchers generally use cluster sampling. In *cluster sampling*, a researcher first divides the population into several large groupings, known as *clusters*. A *cluster* is often defined geographically, such as a county, city, or election district. From there, the researcher can use either simple random or systematic sampling to select the actual persons to be interviewed. Overall, the selection of subjects and the issue of measurement are designed to produce the valid and reliable observations for the researcher to study. The same criteria apply to the remaining methods of data collection.

UNOBTRUSIVE MEASURES

Unlike most other forms of data collection, unobtrusive measures offer the researcher the opportunity to study human behavior without "intruding" on that behavior. In most other instances, subjects are aware that they are being studied. This awareness may lead them to act differently than they would if they were not being observed. This is often known as the "guinea pig" effect.

Unobtrusive measures are any method of data collection that "directly removes the researcher from the set of interactions, events, or behaviors being investigated" (Nachmias & Nachmias, 1976). While there are several types of unobtrusive measures, the type most relevant to public relations is archival records.

Archival records include everything from public documents, such as judicial proceedings and mass media, to private records, such as letters and diaries.

Content Analysis

The systematic study of archival records is called *content analysis*. Content analysis is the second most widely used method of data collection in research on public relations. About 20% of all published PR studies from the past 10 years used this data collection technique. Its primary purpose is to describe a message or set of messages. Professor Ole R. Holsti (1968) defines *content analysis* as, "any technique for making inferences by systematically and objectively identifying specified characteristics of messages."

In public relations, content analysis is used for a variety of purposes. Content analysis can be used to determine everything from the news agenda in local newspaper to content themes in a company newsletter. University researchers Klaus Krippendorff and Michael F. Eleey (1986) suggest that media content analysis can even help to improve strategy effectiveness. Their data reveal differences in media usage of news releases from the Public Broadcasting Corporation depending on program type. This research suggests using alternative strategies to increase coverage of certain broadcasts.

Lerbinger (1977) suggests that it is often used to audit communication activities in corporate settings. For example, researchers might use a form of content analysis known as a *readability study*.

Readability Studies

A readability study helps tell the communicator whether his or her message is written at the right educational level for its audience. Typical readability measures include the Flesch Formula, the FOG Index, and the SMOG Index. They are based primarily upon a count of the number of syllables in a passage in the text. The greater the number of syllables, the more difficult the passage.

Readability measures have been criticized for providing only crude measures of "reading ease." Nevertheless, they offer easy and inexpensive methods for monitoring communications.

As in survey research, the issues of measurement and "subject" selection are of primary importance.

In content analysis, the researcher is first faced with the task of selecting a unit of analysis to measure. The most frequently used units in public relations are: words or terms, themes, and items. A word or term is the smallest unit of analysis. A researcher might use this unit when studying newspaper content to determine the frequency of mention of a particular organization.

Themes provide a broader unit of analysis. They might be used by a researcher for a large manufacturer to determine the frequency of media references to "the environment."

Entire items are the broadest unit. They refer to complete messages, such as a story or photograph. An item analysis might be conducted by a researcher for the National Rifle Association concerned about the frequency of newspaper editorials opposing or supporting gun control.

Once the unit of analysis has been determined, the researcher must develop a system of categorization. This is the process of classifying the units. Typical categories in content analysis include (Holsti, 1968):

(1) Subject matter—What is the communication about?

(2) Direction—How is the subject matter treated (e.g., favorable-unfavorable; strong-weak)?
(3) Conflict—What are the sources and levels of conflict?
(4) Form or type of communication—What is the medium of communication (e.g., newspaper, radio, television)?

Throughout this process, the primary concern is measurement validity and reliability, just as in survey research. The researcher must be sure that his or her classification system does in fact measure what it purports to measure, and that it does so consistently.

"Subject" selection in content analysis begins with a definition of the population under study. Is the focus of the study on internal communications or external? What time period are we concerned about? These are just two of the important questions to consider.

After defining the population, the researcher must decide whether to use a census or a sample of the population. Typically, PR research focuses on sample data, rather than census data. The logic and reasons for this are the same as those for the heavy reliance on sample data in survey research. Similarly, the types of samples are largely the same in content analysis and survey research. Finally, it is important to remember that content analysis is useful only as a descriptive tool. While one can make inferences from content samples to the broader content population, content analysis does not allow the researcher to draw conclusions about cause-and-effect relationships. Sending a message does not guarantee its being received or processed in the desired fashion. This "hypodermic needle" model of communication effects was disproved almost 50 years ago. Thus, PR researchers must use more powerful research techniques to demonstrate the impact of their programs. This leads us to the third broad method of data collection, observational methods.

OBSERVATIONAL METHODS

Observation is the foundation of modern social science. Anthropologists observe simple societies, social psychologists observe small group interaction. From these observations, theories are developed and our understanding of human behavior is increased.

Research on public relations is also founded on observation. The methods discussed thus far are ways of observing human behavior. Surveys and content analyses provide a glimpse of human behavior or its products. They represent, however, indirect methods of observation.

Surveys are based on someone's reported behavior or feeling. Content analysis examines an artifact of human behavior, not the behavior itself.

Observational methods are those data collection techniques that provide a direct measure of human behavior. They range from casual observation of persons in their natural environment to controlled observation in a laboratory environment. Neither method is widely used in systematic research on public relations. Only about 11% of all published PR studies from the past 10 years used either method.

Our review of all research published in *Public Relations Review* since 1976 reveals that only six studies used controlled observation in a laboratory environment (Pavlik & Summerall, 1986). Rarely do PR researchers regularly employ even casual observational methods.

TESTING CAUSATION

The paucity of systematic research of this type in public relations is especially problematic because it is the only approach that offers true tests of cause-and-effect relationships. Thus, almost all research on public relations is limited to description or "correlation." *Correlational studies* are ones that focus on the extent to which two or more variables tend to vary together. For example, Pavlik, Ike E. Nwosu, and Diana Ettel-Gonzales (1982) examined cross-section survey data and found a significant positive correlation between employee career aspirations and company newsletter readership. This study shows that the higher an employee's level of career aspirations, the higher his or her readership level of the company newsletter. Researchers cannot say anything about whether career aspirations cause higher readership, or vice versa. They can only conclude that they are related.

Observational methods offer many ways to test causal relationships. These include laboratory experimentation, field experimentation, and simulations. Laboratory experimentation is the most controlled method of data collection in the social sciences. It allows the researcher to introduce conditions into a simulated natural environment (laboratory) to study their effect on the participants. The work of social psychologist Solomon Asch (1958) on interpersonal influence provides a classic example of laboratory experimentation. This research demonstrates the two primary advantages of laboratory experimentation: rigorous control over both internal and external variables and clear evidence about cause and effect. As in Asch's work, the researcher manipulates the conditions in a laboratory experiment. Similarly, the researcher is able to eliminate the effects of all variables other than the one under study. Thus, the research can draw strong conclusions as to how the variables under study are causally related. Researchers call this the problem of *internal validity*.

The major weakness of laboratory experimentation is its artificial nature. Although a cause-and-effect relationship may hold under highly controlled laboratory conditions, there is considerable reason to doubt that it will hold in the real world—where many other variables come into play. Researchers call this the problem of *external validity*. Field experimentation solves the problem of external validity. By moving into a field setting, the researcher is able to test a cause-and-effect relationship under real-world conditions. Unfortunately, this is at the expense of internal validity. No longer can the researcher state conclusively that "X causes Y." In research, there is always a tradeoff.

A classic example of field experimentation comes from the area of employee relations. Sociologists Lester Coch and John R. P. French (1948) studied why production workers tended to show a high level of resistance to change in methods and jobs, and what could be done to reduce this resistance. Rather than use a controlled laboratory experiment, the researchers chose to go into the workplace and introduce certain conditions. They manipulated workers' level of participation in decision making about the changes. Some workers were allowed no participation, some representative participation, and others total participation. Coch and French found that those employees with the highest level of participation (i.e., total participation) showed no resistance to the changes. Those with no participation showed strong resistance, and those with representative participation had a mild level of resistance.

While the Coch and French study clearly suggests that participation in decision making reduces resistance to change, one cannot be sure that some other environmental factor may have been involved. For example, the level of communication among employees with high or low participation may have differed and may have been the true causal agent.

Burson-Marsteller (Kirban, 1983) is a leading agency that makes strong use of field experimentation. Their program, Audience Impact and Diagnostics (AID), is an in-house effort and deals with everything from consumer product publicity to corporate and issue advertising. Using a quasi-experimental design with pre- and posttest measurements, AID has provided evidence of increased brand awareness, favorable corporate reputation, and interest in the product.

A growing number of field experiments involve the use of multiple methods of data collection. Numerous public information campaigns, for example, incorporate survey research in field experimentation. This "hybrid" offers a promising avenue for research on public relations. Its advantages are primarily the combination of the control of field experimentation and the inexpensiveness of survey research. The disadvantage is that survey research is an indirect form of observation, rather than a direct form. Professors Mark Larson and Karen Massetti-Miller (1984), for example, used survey research in a before-and-after evaluation to measure the effectiveness of a public education campaign. Their evaluation demonstrates that the "War on Waste" anti-pollution campaign successfully influenced public behavior.

Simulations represent a third observational method for testing cause-and-effect relationships. They can be computer simulations, games (person simulations), and person-computer simulations. The major advantage of simulations is that they allow the researcher easy manipulation of conditions. For example, computer specialists Joseph Harper and Wayne Danielson (1986) have developed a newspaper management computer simulation. Their simulation allows the user to manipulate a variety of economic factors, such as the cost of news print, the number of full-time employees, or circulation, to study the impact on profits.

Simulations have rarely been used in the study of public relations. A review of the published research on public relations reveals only a handful of studies in this area, most of which study the usefulness of simulations as an educational device (Hunt, 1985; Pavlik, 1986).

After collecting the data, the researcher conducts a data analysis using statistical tools. While a full discussion of these tools is highly technical and beyond the scope of this book, we can discuss some of the major issues involved.

Generally speaking, there are two types of statistics: descriptive and inferential. Descriptive statistics are used to simplify and summarize large and complex sets of data. Typical statistics include the mean (or average) and the range, which tells us how the data are spread out.

Inferential statistics are used to make generalizations from a sample to a broader population. Typical statistics include the t-test (for examining differences between measures) and the correlation (for examining relationships between measures). Inferential statistics can be used only on data obtained through probability sampling techniques, while descriptive statistics can be used on any type of sample.

SUMMARY

Overall, systematic research on public relations has tended to use the scientific method as a means for generating knowledge. Its focus is on empirical research, research based on systematic observations of events and processes in the environment.

Data collection methods come primarily from the social sciences, with heavy use made of survey research and unobtrusive methods, especially content analysis. As a cost-saving device, most published surveys on public relations have relied upon mail questionnaires. Unfortunately, this means that response rates have been poor, and the generalizability of the results is cast in doubt.

Observational methods such as laboratory or field experimentation have been rare. These methods, which allow the only true tests of causal relationships, are expensive.

Data are analyzed using descriptive and inferential statistics.

In public relations, researchers need to move away from the heavy use of survey research and toward a greater reliance on other methods, especially observational methods. Perhaps more important, there needs to be a move toward cross-validation of findings. We need to begin testing ideas and collecting information via multiple methods—collect survey data in one study, unobtrusive in another, and observational in a third. This approach will help build a stronger knowledge base for the profession of public relations. It will do this by demonstrating the validity and reliability of the research.

3

MAJOR RESEARCH FINDINGS

We have learned a great deal from the systematic study of public relations, including knowledge that is both theoretical and problem oriented.

Most of the published research about public relations to date is designed to help improve the practice of public relations. The primary scholarly journal of the field, *Public Relations Review*, stresses applied research. Thus, the journal intones, "Articles should reflect high standards of scholarship as well as practical applications to public relations." This goal has set a clear agenda for the research questions addressed. The bulk of these published studies are what we call *strategic research*.

STRATEGIC RESEARCH

Strategic research is also of central importance to those conducting proprietary research. This is reflected in the comments of Michael Rowan (1986), who leads the world's largest PR research operation, a subsidiary of Hill & Knowlton. He reports that one of the first changes he made was to "stop conducting research for publicity purposes, and start using it for strategic purposes." This is also his principal basis for changing the name of the agency from "Group Attitudes Corporation" to "Strategic Information Research Corporation."

Studying PR Tools and Techniques

Not surprisingly, much of the strategic research undertaken has focused on studying the tools and techniques used in the practice of public relations. Some studies examine methods that have been used in the past, while others suggest new techniques. Before discussing the specific studies that have been conducted, let's briefly examine the major tools and techniques used by PR practitioners. This examination will help provide a framework for organizing our review of the research. The tools include editorial services, corporate advertising, publicity, news conferences, special events, fund-raising, audiovisual techniques, speech writing, and lobbying. Of these areas, editorial services probably has served as the focus of the largest number of studies examining public relations tools and techniques, followed by corporate advertising, and audiovisual techniques.

Editorial Services

The tools and techniques most typically associated with public relations fall under the heading of *editorial services*, which involves writing, editing, publications, and press relations. Jan Van Meter, Senior Vice President of Hill & Knowlton, in 1984 writes that an editorial services department should be "capable of delivering high-quality work" in areas ranging from internal communications (including employee newsletters and magazines) to news releases to annual reports.

A 1976 article by Professor Craig E. Aronoff, published in *Public Relations Review*, provides a good example of research on editorial services. Aronoff's article, "Predictors of Success in Placing Releases in Newspapers," examines data from a survey of newspaper editors. His data reveal that "news releases from local sources . . . were very likely to be accepted. Such releases were likely to come from sources from whom the gatekeeper has received releases previously and often, and with whom the gatekeeper might well have a personal acquaintance." The releases, Aronoff adds, "are likely to be perceived as objective and of medium importance and interest." Aronoff's study also indicates that PR people are often seen as extensions of the newspaper staff—with information being exchanged routinely and with a high level of trust. Similarly, gatekeepers are more likely to publish a release from a PR source they know on a personal level.

A number of other related studies have followed Aronoff's. One particularly interesting study is reported by political scientist Norman R. Luttbeg (1983). Luttbeg's study is of particular interest because its findings directly contradict those of Aronoff's. He conducted a systematic content analysis of 100 newspapers selected randomly from *Editor and Publisher's* listing of all American dailies. Based on an analysis of 1980-1981 data, Luttbeg found no bias for stories "closer to home." He reports, "Papers covering a story on average are two miles closer than those omitting coverage." According to professors Roy E. Carter and Warren J. Mitovsky (1961), "perceived distances, which are a function of regional or cultural similarities may be more important than actual distance (Luttbeg, 1983)." Luttbeg (1983) concludes that "proximity [coming from a local source] does not assure newsworthiness."

Similar results are reported in an unpublished study conducted in 1985 by William Mahon of the Public Information Office of the Pennsylvania State University. Mahon's study examines the coverage of Pennsylvania's five largest public research universities in four large circulation daily newspapers in the state. His content analysis reveals that the Pennsylvania State University (PSU) received coverage equal to or greater than that of any other school, even in their hometowns. For example, PSU received more extensive coverage in the *Philadelphia Inquirer* than either the University of Pennsylvania or Temple—despite the fact that both these schools are located in Philadelphia and the main campus of PSU is more than 150 miles away. It's worth noting as well that Mahon's study *excluded* all football coverage, since including coverage of the 11-1 exploits of Joe Paterno's Nittany Lion football team would have made "the score" even more lopsided in favor of PSU. Overall, Mahon's study suggests that many other factors may be at least as important as the local angle. These include economic importance of the institution being covered, size of the institution, and even writing style of the press release.

Research by professors Bruce Vanden Bergh, Alan D. Fletcher, and Mary A. Adrian (1984) reveals a new medium for external PR communications. Their survey identifies the local business press as a key vehicle for reaching the business community, especially business management. These publications are neither newspapers nor magazines, but offer the affluent reader as their greatest asset. Readers have a median income of $60,000-$70,000, and an average income of more than $100,000. The publications are limited to local business news, but have varying editorial content and style. Some have a newspaper format, while others have a glossy, magazine appearance. Vanden Bergh et al. show that these publications have high reader involvement, which makes them especially attractive to advertisers and PR communicators. Circulation ranges from less than 15,000 (e.g., the *Pacific Business News* in Hawaii) to more than 35,000 (e.g., Crain's *Chicago Business*). The number of these publications has increased dramatically in recent years; there were 14 publications listed in 1980 by the Association of American Business Publications and 60 listed in 1984. On the down side, these highly specialized publications tend to have a high cost per thousand (cpm) readers.

Editorial services embraces not only external communications, but internal communications, as well. Employee communications has been one of the favorite topics for research investigations. Exxon's *The Lamp* was the focus of one such study by Professor Mary Ann Ferguson-DeThorne (1978). Her content analysis reveals that *The Lamp* performed poorly during the 1970s as a vehicle for informing employees of the impending oil shortage and possible energy conservation methods. It was slow to bring messages to its employee audience, which may explain *The Lamp*'s credibility problems, Ferguson-DeThorne suggests.

A survey by researchers Stuart H. Surlin and Barry Walker (1975) shows that employees strongly favor in-depth coverage of such "bad" news by a company newspaper, but don't expect to get it.

Professors Dennis W. Jeffers and David N. Bateman (1980) thus contend that the time has come to move corporate magazines out of the "soft arena" of corporate affairs, by dealing with hard issues that may not always involve "good" news. They recommend developing specific objectives for corporate communications and measuring the effectiveness of these efforts. Despite the growing recognition of the need to change employee communications, recent reports indicate that employee communications may be in trouble. A mail survey by organizational researchers Brian S. Morgan and William A. Schiemann (1983) shows that employees believe that they are not kept well-informed, that management is not willing to listen to them, and that they have to rely on the grapevine for information. Employees want information directly from supervisors and top-level management.

Employee newsletters offer the potential to fill this communication gap. Management, however, must be willing to take the time to sit down and listen to employees periodically to learn about their needs and concerns. A survey by Professor Ronald Goodman and management consultant Richard S. Ruch (1982) reveals that news of senior management influenced workers' job attitudes more than any other single factor. CEOs must make a commitment to the "Doctrine of Open Communications."

Annual reports represent another important product of internal editorial services. A series of recent investigations (Haskins, 1984; Heath & Phelps, 1984) shows that annual reports are the most complex and difficult to read of any PR communications. This is neither surprising nor necessarily a problem, however, given the function of the annual report. Since its primary audience is the financial community, it need not be tailored to a general population. Still, when done well, an annual report is more than a financial document. It can be both a PR and marketing tool; it can be used in employee relations, as a recruiting tool, or even as a visual representation of the whole organization. Thus, shorter sentences, less complicated diction, and better use of graphics will enhance the effectiveness of the corporate annual report.

A recent mail survey (*Public Relations Journal*, 1984b) indicates a troubling if not alarming finding about the investor community's perception of corporate annual reports. This survey found that many individual and professional investors tend to distrust what they read in annual reports. They believe that bad news and problems are often hidden or omitted. Richard E. Cheney, Chairman, USA Hill & Knowlton, observes (*Public Relations Journal*, 1984b), "These findings show that gaining the investor's trust is still the biggest problem for the annual report."

Computers are emerging as a new medium for internal corporate communications (as well as external communications). A survey by practitioners Martha C. Glenn, William H. Gruber, and Kenneth H. Rabin (1982) shows that while corporate awareness of this new medium has increased, the actual number using the computer as a communication tool is still relatively small. Of those that do use the computer, they are able to develop and maintain mailing lists more efficiently; store, retrieve, and update speeches, press releases, and other communications; monitor the status of legislative reports (using Lexis); and access other data bases. They are even experimenting with the two-way interactive potential of the networked personal computer in corporate communications.

Corporate Advertising

Researchers have also been giving more attention to the increasingly important area of corporate advertising. A study by marketing Professors Charles H. Patti and John P. McDonald, published in a 1985 issue of the *Journal of Advertising*, reported that the importance of corporate advertising has increased significantly in the past 15 years and will continue to do so for at least the remainder of the decade. The *Public Relations Journal*'s thirteenth annual survey of corporate advertising expenditures in the major mass media (1984b) shows a 13.3% increase in 1983 for companies, and a 26.1% jump for trade associations. In 1975, U.S. corporations and associations spent $305 million on corporate advertising in the major media. In 1984, they spent more than $1 billion.

Heading the list of corporate advertisers is AT&T, with more than $72 million in expenditures in 1984. An unexpected sixth on this list is the Reagan Presidential Committee, with almost $22 million in 1984 expenditures! The media, in order of 1984 corporate advertising expenditures, are television, radio, newspapers, magazines, and outdoor.

Patti and McDonald (1985), based upon a mail survey of the heads of advertising and PR departments for the 500 largest corporations in the United States, report that more than a third (37%) of the respondents say their company's corporate advertising budget increased from the previous year. More than a quarter (28%) say their budget stayed the same. Thus, well less than a third (18%) say their corporate advertising budget decreased (17% did not respond to this question). Numerous other investigations have also been undertaken in this area (e.g., Chase, 1975; Darling, 1975; Sachs, 1981; Sachs & Chasin, 1976, 1977; Sethi, 1983).

Patti and McDonald (1985) argue that four key issues dominate the literature on corporate advertising research:

(1) defining corporate advertising
(2) determining the objectives of corporate advertising and whether they differ from those of product or brand advertising
(3) identifying the target audiences of corporate advertising
(4) measuring the effectiveness of corporate advertising

Defining Corporate Advertising. Little consensus has emerged as to just what corporate advertising is. Thomas F. Garbett (1981), senior vice president at Doyle, Dane, Bernbach (New York), suggests that *corporate advertising* is nothing more than a "catchall term for a type of advertising run for the direct benefit of the corporation rather than for the product or services." This is perhaps an accurate description, but it provides little insight into the function, purpose, or effects of corporate advertising.

Meanwhile many corporate executives offer definitions stated in terms of activities, such as "image building." Patti and McDonald also report that others define it as an outcome, "goodwill." The objective of one typical corporate campaign was "to improve or maintain the company's reputation and goodwill." Professors William Sachs and Joseph Chasin (1977) similarly report little agreement among practitioners as to a working definition of corporate advertising. Further research is clearly needed in this area to help establish both a working and a conceptual definition of the nature of corporate advertising. *Objectives.* If corporate advertising is not designed to sell a company's products or services, what is it designed to do? A number of scholars have recently attempted to answer this question. Few have done so satisfactorily. Thomas J. Fay (1984), vice president of communications for TRW, Inc., believes there are at least two distinct purposes behind corporate advertising. They are to:

(1) call attention to the company and differentiate it from its competitors (this was formerly called *institutional advertising*, but the term has "gone out of vogue")
(2) help solve a problem or ward off a threat by giving the company's point of view on some issue (this is sometimes referred to as *issue advertising* or *advocacy advertising*).

Fay also suggests that most corporate advertising is designed to meet the first purpose, and only occasionally to satisfy the second. Fay's perceptions are confirmed by the findings of Patti and McDonald (1985). Their survey shows that nearly two-thirds of their respondents report that corporate "image" and "identity" are the basis for employing corporate advertising. Almost half even use the term "*institutional*" in describing their view of corporate advertising. Only about a quarter report "issue" or "advocacy" as the primary focus of their company's corporate advertising. Patti and McDonald's study further suggests that the specific objectives for corporate advertising are overwhelmingly (88%) stated in terms of communications. For example, creating awareness of a company's name or position on an issue is a typical communication objective.

Less common are objectives designed to influence attitudes or public opinion—about two-thirds say their objectives include enhancing the company image or changing attitudes about an issue. The smallest number report objectives geared toward changing behavior. Only a third of the respondents in the Patti and McDonald study say their messages are designed to generate inquiries, attract more employees, or otherwise influence behavior. These results are not surprising for at least two reasons. First, the hierarchy of effects model and other attitude theory predicts that behavior change is usually less than and dependent upon communication or knowledge and attitude change. The hierarchy of effects model suggests that there are three principal types of effects attributable to the mass media: communication or knowledge, attitudinal, and behavioral change. Most often, behavior change follows from one or both of the others. Trained in communication, it is not surprising that practitioners would align their corporate advertising objectives with these principles. As a result, PR people have played an important role in the development and implementation of corporate advertising campaigns (O'Brien, 1980; *Public Relations Journal*, 1976a, 1976b, 1977). Second, since corporate advertising is not designed to boost product sales, one would expect it to have more traditional PR objectives. These traditional objectives typically involve establishing a corporate identity, building goodwill, or improving a company's standing with its relevant publics. Often, the message focuses on corporate social responsibility. For instance, messages might be designed to demonstrate that the company is a good citizen—that it undertakes activities to promote the public good. *Target Audiences.* A basic question here is whether companies use corporate advertising to reach the same audiences targeted by other PR efforts or whether these audiences represent different publics. Some contend that corporate advertising is best aimed at the convertibles (Woolward, 1982). *Convertibles* are persons who are not already committed to a position and can be "converted" to the company's point of view.

The survey by Patti and McDonald suggests that corporate advertising often may be targeted more toward traditional advertising audiences than toward PR groups. According to the data, the number one target audience is existing customers, not the typical primary target in public relations. Running close behind is the financial community and prospective customers. Shareholders, employees, and other special publics—which often head the list of key audiences for other PR efforts—are way down the list of target audiences for corporate advertising.

In general, Sachs (1981) reports, the commercial goals of the corporate advertising campaign are the chief determinants of the target audience.

Practitioner William Latshaw (1977) suggests that target group research is an effective technique in corporate advertising, especially for advocacy advertising. His research shows significant differences in attitudes among magazine readership. Through careful analysis, the corporate advertiser can buy precise market segments defined by their attitudes. Thus the corporate advertising message can be tailored to different groups. One can also reach the maximum number of a specific attitudinal target group at a lower cost, with known frequency of exposure (i.e., number of times).

Research suggests, then, that corporate advertising is aptly named. It is a tool that seems to bridge the gap between public relations and marketing. Its messages are not designed to sell goods or services, but its audiences are existing and prospective customers. Surveys by the *Public Relations Journal* (1976b, 1977) indicate that PR people often play a major role in shaping corporate advertising policies and practices. PR executives are involved in the advertising conception, theme, budget, and media selection. Typically, PR departments are the principal originators of the concepts for corporate advertising.

Measuring Effectiveness

A number of studies (Grass, 1977; *Public Relations Journal*, 1979; Reeves & Ferguson-DeThorne, 1980; Sachs & Chasin, 1977) have addressed the issue of corporate advertising effectiveness. Research consistently shows that effectiveness is more accurately determined when specific, rather than general, measures are used. For example, DuPont moved away from general measures of how favorably the public views the company, to specific measures of changes in belief and evaluation as revealed in controlled laboratory exposure to DuPont corporate advertising (Grass, 1977). This research demonstrates that corporate advertising can change people's beliefs about a company— but there is still no answer to how much that change in belief is worth in financial terms. Furthermore, other research (*Public Relations Journal*, 1979) shows that corporate advertising cannot be relied upon alone to build a corporate image. Still, research shows that corporate advertising can influence the perceptions and attitudes of affluent, well-educated target audiences (Grass, 1977).

Publicity

Publicity is probably the most widely visible tool of public relations. In the late 1800s, P. T. Barnum effectively used publicity to shape public perceptions and opinion. In recent years, however, it has been the impact of negative publicity that has caused the greatest concern to practitioners of public relations. Witness some events of the 1980s.

1981: Procter & Gamble recalls its Rely tampon when the product is linked to toxic shock syndrome. The result: a financial loss of $75 million and substantial negative publicity for Procter & Gamble. *1982*: Johnson & Johnson withdraws Extra Strength Tylenol, after product tampering leads to the deaths of seven persons in the Chicago area. The result: a loss of $50 million, plus seriously damaging negative publicity.

1984: Union Carbide closes its pesticide manufacturing plant in Bhopal, India, after a poisonous gas leak kills more than 2,000 persons. The result: a financial loss that may reach the billions of dollars when all law suits are settled, and months of front-page negative publicity—enough to threaten the existence of Union Carbide.

Consequently, PR researchers have begun exploring the impact of negative publicity on public attitudes. In one such recent study (1985), the academic research team of Daniel Sherrell, R. Eric Reidenbach, Ellen Moore, Jay Wagle, and Thaddeus Spratlin explored the impact of negative publicity on consumer attitudes toward Johnson & Johnson in the aftermath of the 1982 Tylenol-tampering incident. Using evidence from a four-city survey, Sherrell et al. concluded that the impact of negative publicity on consumer attitudes is likely to be greater than the impact of "overdoses" of positive information. The authors suggest that a set of specific response strategies is the most effective method of handling negative publicity situations. They recommend working closely with the marketing personnel to "take responsibility publicly" for the problem while mounting a campaign to restore confidence in the company's products.

Audiovisual Techniques

A fourth major area of research on PR tools involves the study of audiovisual techniques. These investigations range from experiments on the impact of videotaped corporate messages to surveys about the new phenomenon of the video news release (Clavier & Kalupa, 1983; Rubin, 1985).

Although many television and radio stations are less inclined to use public service announcements (PSAs) now that the Federal Communications Commission (FCC) has relaxed its legal pressure to do so, PSAs are still an important PR tool. Two recent studies (Goodman, 1981; Smith & Rabin, 1978) looked at the factors that affect the likelihood of obtaining PSA air time. The researchers surveyed by mail public affairs directors at television and radio stations and identified several important issues. First, PSAs to be aired on local stations should address local concerns, involve reputable sponsoring agencies, and follow the 30-second format. In radio, it should be noted that celebrity voices do not assure air time. In addition, direct appeals for money will reduce the chances of getting a PSA aired.

As an alternative to PSAs, I-and-I programming should be considered as a vehicle for reaching the general public through the broadcast media (Turow & Park, 1981). *I-and-I* refers to information and interview programming. Access to these programs is usually easy—and does not involve expensive production costs. Unfortunately, they are usually scheduled during low-ratings time slots, and thus generate small audiences. This, however, has plagued PSAs, too. Similarly, video news releases (VNRs) have emerged as an effective mechanism for obtaining air time during local news programming, as a survey by *Public Relations Journal* reporter Alissa Rubin (1985) reveals. Her mail survey indicates that approximately 90% of all U.S. markets are using VNRs, with many being distributed via satellite.

A number of experiments have been conducted in order to determine the factors that influence the persuasiveness of an audiovisual communication, especially source credibility (e.g., Clavier & Kalupa, 1983; Lynn, Wyatt, Gaines, Pearce, & Vanden Bergh, 1978). An experiment by Professors David E. Clavier and Frank B. Kalupa (1983) involved controlled exposure to an Illinois Power Co. rebuttal videotape to a *60 Minutes* investigative piece. In the *60 Minutes* piece, Illinois Power was portrayed as being incompetent in the construction of a nuclear power facility. Illinois Power produced a rebuttal tape in which the *60 Minutes* version was compared with an Illinois Power version. Illinois Power had videotaped the entire *60 Minutes* interview. Illinois Power's goal was to show the bias and inaccuracies of the *60 Minutes* story. An experiment was set up involving college student subjects. Students were randomly assigned to three different treatment groups: (1) Some saw only the Illinois Power rebuttal; (2) some saw only the *60 Minutes* story; and (3) some saw both versions. The experiment produced at least two important results. First, the most dramatic effect was that exposure to the rebuttal significantly lowered the credibility of the original news source, *60 Minutes*. Second, it confirmed that credibility is not a one-dimensional concept—it is more than trustworthiness. In this case, "expertise" was the critical factor—Illinois Power was seen as much more expert than the *60 Minutes* source, although it was seen as trustworthy.

In contrast, a similar experiment by Professors Carolyn G. Cline and Lynne Masel-Waters (1984) found a backlash effect of a corporate videotape. In this experiment, an Illinois Bell-produced videotape generated negative attitudes toward AT&T—a backlash effect. The researchers recommend carefully pretesting videotapes—and studying the target audience. Audiences that are not already committed to the organization being promoted may interpret the information presented in order to fit their existing beliefs—rather than change their beliefs.

Finally, studies have looked at the use of photographs in PR messages. Professor Linda P. Morton (1985) shows through laboratory research that readers respond favorably to photographs. In fact, many studies have shown that photographs are often the "most read" (Pavlik et al., 1982). Photographs get attention and can effectively reinforce a verbal message.

Psychographics

One of the newest tools of public relations is called *psychographics*. Originally designed for advertisers, it is a method of segmenting audiences. One well-known psychographics model was put together in the mid-1970s by SRI International, a Menlo Park, California-based think tank (Zotti, 1985). The Values and Lifestyles Program (VALS) divides people into nine categories, from poor, barely coping sustainers and survivors, to "enviable integrateds, who have managed to combine affluence with spiritual fulfillment to achieve the ultimate lifestyle."

While the VALS program is expensive, a number of leading PR agencies have started using it. Examples include Ketchum PR and Burson-Marsteller for the National Turkey Federation. "One of the ways psychographics is most useful is as a conceptual tool," reports Charlotte Vogel, president of The Research Group, a consulting firm for PR planning and evaluation (Zotti, 1985). She continues, "It doesn't necessarily have to be a formal piece of research, it can force more consciousness of the need to focus on who you're really talking to in the programs that you do, and that's a big problem in public relations."

Program Areas

Beyond the tools and techniques of public relations, researchers have studied many of the key program areas of the field. These include studies of media relations, international public relations, and politics and public relations.

Management

One of the most important new program areas of public relations is management (Brody, 1985). According to John Beardsley (1986), chief executive officer at Padilla & Speer, a leading Minneapolis-based agency, "Now that public relations is part of management—we must be able to speak their language. Public relations is part of management science and the more we know about the science of communication, the more effective we will be." As public relations has moved into the management sphere, a number of concerns have emerged, including issues management, crisis management, human resource management, and management styles. Issues management is an emerging function in many organizations (Ehling & Hesse, 1983). It represents an "alternative to the traditional approach to public policy concerns by allowing for advanced planning, at least on emerging issues (Shelby, 1986)." In this sense, issues management is linked to the agenda-setting function of the media. Issues management, like agenda setting, focuses on the emergence of public issues and their relevant attributes.

What does research tell us about issues management? Examining the research to date reveals at least three main areas of concern: first, defining the function of issues management; second, defining the process of issues management; and, third, managing the process. Several practitioner surveys (e.g., Ehling & Hesse, 1983; Shelby, 1984) have been undertaken to define the function of issues management. The most important finding is that there is no consensus about the exact nature of issues management—it can be defined differently in every organization. One survey respondent (Shelby, 1984) described the function as a vehicle to "alert top management, determine priorities, and recommend policy." Another saw it as a way to "maximize accuracy and credibility of the company's position."

Professor Annette N. Shelby (1986) contends that "theoretically, at least, issues management aims for a positive, pro-active response to emerging issues that will have probable and significant impact on the organization." Further research will be needed to determine whether and how quickly this theoretical definition becomes the working definition in the field.

Although the function of issues management is unclear, the process is fairly well defined. Most practitioners subscribe to the Chase-Jones model (Shelby, 1986). It embraces the following five steps: (1) issue identification, (2) analysis, (3) action plans, (4) implementation, and (5) evaluation of results.

The critical stage in this process is the identification of issues. Paradoxically, this is also the most often neglected. Typically, issues are identified through environmental monitoring and scanning. One survey (University of Florida, 1983) reveals that more than half the respondents always use these techniques, while most sometimes use them. Unfortunately, the approach used is often more informal than systematic. Other issue identification procedures are trend impact analysis and trend extrapolation. Use of these techniques is fairly expensive and requires a fairly high level of sophistication in quantitative analysis.

Managing the process is the third important area of issues management. There is, however, little systematic research on this element in the PR field. What is known from outside public relations—issues management has been used for about 20 years in government and business—is that issues management is generally a somewhat linear, sequential process in which public opinion is the first step, and regulation and litigation form the last step.

Emerging is an alternative view in which the impetus comes from within an organization, rather than from the outside environment. This may represent the "ultimate" in issues management. It may also reflect the fears of issues management critic Richard A. Armstrong, former president of the Public Affairs Council. He said (1981) the term "carries implications of manipulation and arrogance and it sounds very self-serving. Issues cannot be managed."

Crisis management, an area of vital importance in public relations, has received little systematic research attention to date. Rather, individual case studies have dominated the literature. For example, Leonard Snyder (1983), an independent researcher with The 2nd Opinion Co., offered a critique of Johnson & Johnson's handling of the Tylenol crisis. While such case analyses are useful, systematic investigations are needed to move our understanding beyond the level of personal opinion and into the realm of scientific knowledge.

Plant closings have been studied as an aspect of crisis management. A quarterly survey of corporate executives' perceptions of the "sudden impact" of this crisis issue was recently reported in the *Corporate Issues Monitor* (Gorney, 1985). More than half the 105 Fortune 500 companies' senior public affairs and PR executives say two to six months is a realistic amount of time their companies could give communities before closing a plant. This does not leave much time to establish an effective plan of action. How to handle plant closings is an important issue that remains to be studied systematically.

Human resource management is of increasing importance, and recent survey research reflects this. More than half the respondents in a mail survey of PRSA members say their organizations are using human resource management (Nickerson, Schuster, & Murdick, 1982). Respondents report this is critical in an era of decreasing productivity and increasing desire for worker participation in organizational decision making.

Human resource management stresses the need for open, two-way communication between management and employees. The value of such communication can be dramatic, as a recent survey reveals. "Companies that conduct employee attitude surveys are far less likely to have labor strikes than companies that don't," reports Robert J. Aiello (1983), senior vice president, Ketchum Public Relations (Pittsburgh). A Ketchum survey of 50 Fortune 500 companies shows that of unionized companies that use attitude surveys, only a quarter had strikes in the last six years. In contrast, of those that do not use surveys, almost half had strikes in this period. Aiello concludes that attitude surveys are influencing corporate decision making and helping to "locate employee unrest before it broadens into work stoppages."

Media Relations

One of the most fundamental relationships in public relations is that between practitioners and the media. To a large extent, members of each field are mutually dependent. PR people depend on the media to distribute their messages to members of the public. Journalists and other media practitioners rely on PR sources for information and access to business and other organizations. We could call this relationship a symbiotic one.

Yet, there has often been a fairly high level of conflict between these two groups (Aronoff, 1975; Evans, 1984; Finn, 1981; Kopenhaver, Martinson, & Ryan, 1984). They have not always worked smoothly together. For example, journalists have often accused PR people of withholding information. Conversely, PR people have sometimes charged the journalistic community with having a "liberal bias," or being one-sided in reporting.

What does systematic research tell us about this relationship? First of all, a number of content analyses show that media coverage of business has been fairly evenhanded—if not positive (Hynds, 1980; University of Minnesota, 1979). A study in the General Motors report on business and the news media reveals that more than 80% of the Twin Cities' press coverage of business is neutral or positive (University of Minnesota, 1979). Fewer than one in five stories has a negative slant. This has been confirmed in other studies, including media coverage of the Three-Mile Island Nuclear Incident (Stephens & Edison, 1982). A 1980 study by Professor Ernest C. Hynds also shows that business coverage is improving—that the media are increasingly aware of the need to cover business well and they are devoting more space to this coverage. Businesspersons also tend to have a favorable view of business coverage (Rippey, 1981), although there are some weaknesses.

Still, tension exists between members of business and the media, PR practitioners and journalists. In the mid-1970s, a national survey by Aronoff (1975) revealed that journalists and PR practitioners differed widely in their views of each other. For instance, most practitioners disagreed with the following statement: PR practitioners try to deceive journalists by attaching too much importance to unimportant events. In contrast, almost all journalists agreed with this statement.

Since the Aronoff study, a number of more recent surveys have uncovered an interesting shift in this tension. The American Management Association commissioned one revealing study by David Finn (1981), a leading PR counselor. Finn looked at the business-media relationship and found a high level of misconception and resulting distrust. His survey of PR executives shows that almost three-fourths (73%) of the executives "believe reporters don't accurately research their topics." More than half (63%) say "reporters play on public emotions." They also believe reporting inaccuracies are not due to bias, but merely sloppiness.

Meanwhile, most journalists (60%) "feel business executives are defensive and don't give reporters a chance to question them." The same portion feel that "business people are not honest with their own PR departments."

Other studies show that neither journalists nor PR practitioners hold the very strong negative views of each other that we often heard about 10 years ago. Rather, there tends to be a fairly high level of mutual respect—journalists tend to think most PR people do a good job and vice versa (Baker, 1977; Brody, 1984; University of Minnesota, 1979). Further, members of each group tend to hold the same news values. One survey (Jeffers, 1977) even showed that PR people overestimate the skills and ethics of journalists.

The tension seems to be a product of a set of misperceptions held by each group or of misunderstandings (Kopenhaver, 1985; University of Minnesota, 1979). For instance, journalists tend to overestimate the extent to which PR people are critical of journalists. Similarly, PR people tend to overestimate the extent to which journalists agree with criticisms of public relations. This often produces a defensive mind-set. The reasons for these misperceptions are many, including a simple lack of knowledge, as well as journalism higher education, which has not tended to give an accurate picture of the PR profession (Cline, 1982). The University of Minnesota study (1979) concludes that this tension may be healthy—it encourages members of each group to maintain a critical eye in the communication process.

Meanwhile, Grunig's research (1982) leads him to call for establishing a dialogue between journalists and public relations people. His research has uncovered a fairly significant lack of knowledge of business—an economic illiteracy (Barlow & Kaufmann, 1975)—among journalists. He recommends developing economic education programs for the press.

This same concept can be applied to other areas of public relations, as well. For example, research indicates that PR people play a vital role in the reporting of science (Dunwoody & Ryan, 1983). Journalists want and need direct access to the scientists themselves, and scientists prefer the direct contact with journalists as well (Strasser, 1978). The role of the PR practitioner, then, is one of mediator between members of these groups. Understanding the media goes beyond an examination of PR practitioner and journalist attitudes. It requires an examination of public attitudes toward the media, uses of the media, and the changing nature of the media and new technology. The following discussion reviews key findings in these areas.

Research tells us that the public has a high level of confidence in the media (Izard, 1985). Although there had been a drop-off in public confidence in most social institutions—including the mass media and support institutions such as public relations—there has been a resurgence in the 1980s. Research also tells us that people typically use the mass media for entertainment purposes. Grunig's research (1979a), for example, shows that low involvement, consummatory media use is the most prevalent, while high involvement, functional use is somewhat rare. This has several clear implications for public relations, especially in the area of campaign planning. Specifically, it suggests that messages for the general public must be simple, emotional ones that can capture attention. Only under conditions of high audience involvement—which are rare—can complex messages be communicated effectively.

There are also important differences in the way people use different media. Numerous studies have repeatedly shown that newspapers are the dominant source of information about state government and local news (Reagan & Ducey, 1983). Similarly, those who prefer newspapers as a source of news tend to be more knowledgeable (Hofstetter, Zirkin, & Bass, 1978; Reagan & Ducey, 1983). Television, however, has emerged as the dominant entertainment medium (Comstock, Chaffee, Katzman, McCombs, & Roberts, 1978). It is also the principal source of national news for the general public. A recent Canadian study showed that television news is perceived as more accurate than both newspaper and radio news—by a convincing margin (Wilson & Howard, 1978). In the U.S., this is also the case for older adults (Doolittle, 1979). Public television is also an important medium for certain audiences—primarily the white, more affluent and well-educated audience. One study by Professor Robert L. Stevenson (1979) shows that Blacks in North Carolina and Mississippi are both less aware of public television offerings and watch less public television.

Cable and other telecommunication technologies have emerged as important communication vehicles in our society. A survey by practitioner Kevin Hawkins (1984) suggests that most PR practitioners know very little about these new technologies. Although 95% of 400 PRSA members surveyed said cable will increase in importance, almost half said they had no cable outlets on their media lists. Only 15% reported having more than 10 outlets. Almost two-thirds only rarely use cable outlets in the distribution of messages.

Cable television and other new electronic technologies represent new opportunities for "narrowcasting"—the ability to hit target audiences in an increasingly fragmented marketplace. PR practitioners face the challenge of keeping abreast of these rapidly changing communication technologies. The computer represents an almost untapped communication medium—it has also been the subject of very little systematic research (see Glenn et al., 1982; Harris, Garramone, Pizante, & Komiza, 1985).

Politics and Public Relations

In an era of political image making, public relations has played a major role in many election campaigns (Strand, Dozier, Hofstetter, & Ledingham, 1983). Recent government figures revealed that candidates spent more than $100 million in the 1984 elections. Much of this was for public relations. Research has much to tell us about this process. A number of investigations have shown that mass media messages can exert a significant influence on the electorate (DeBock, 1976; Hurd & Singletary, 1984; McCleneghan, 1980; Mulder, 1979; Patterson & McClure, 1976; St. Dizier, 1985). Professors Thomas E. Patterson and Robert E. McClure (1976) demonstrate significant effects on knowledge from television political advertising exposure in the 1972 presidential election. A study by Professor Byron St. Dizier (1985) shows that when available information about a candidate is minimal, newspaper endorsements can have stronger effects than political party affiliation. Another study (DeBock, 1976) indicates that in a one-sided presidential election, in-state poll reports may cause the underdog to suffer a loss in preference intensity and turnout motivation.

Leading media researcher Steven H. Chaffee (Zhao & Chaffee, 1986) cautions, however, that we must be careful to avoid "rushing to generalizations" about media political effects. In contrast to the Patterson and McClure study of a decade ago, Xinshu Zhao and Chaffee found almost no knowledge gain from exposure to political advertising in the 1984 presidential election. They conclude that media political effects are situational and dependent on many factors, including historical context, the political campaign, and media content. Although sometimes significant, these effects are not uniform. This, of course, is true of the media in general.

Making Sense of Political Communication. Chaffee and John Hochheimer (1985) contend that the view of "the roles of mass communication in the political process has remained largely intact since the earliest major studies conducted in the United States (Lazarsfeld and others, 1944; Berelson and others, 1954)." This view, they argue, is one of "limited effects." Most published studies have focused on cognitive and affective effects, and not the more powerful behavioral effects.

Researchers have employed a "source-message-channel-receiver picture of communication," which some (Dervin, 1980, 1981) believe "puts matters backwards" (Chaffee & Hochheimer, 1985). They believe that people are active creators of their own information, "defined as the sense one makes of the world while moving through time and space" (Chaffee & Hochheimer, 1985). The media act as lenses through which we view the world, and structure it to make sense (Hochheimer, 1982). This person-oriented perspective presents a new view of the political communication process, one that PR communicators may find both challenging and powerful.

Political Advertising. One of the most important tools of the political publicist is the television political spot ad. This tool has been used with increasing frequency in the past decade, at all levels. What does research tell us about the nature of political spot ads? One study (Joslyn, 1980) shows that political ads are most likely to contain information about candidate characteristics—about one-half the ads studied. In contrast, this study also found only one-fifth contain information on the candidate's position on the issues. Clearly, political advertising is designed to build awareness and shape images—not to inform.

A very interesting content-analytic study (Bird, 1985) revealed a stylistic difference between spots for male and female candidates. Spots for female candidates are less likely to stress strength, and more likely to stress compassion.

How effective are political ads? Clearly, political advertising is not a panacea (Garramone, 1984a), but it can be used effectively to build awareness or shape perceptions. A panel study on the effects of televised political ads in the 1975 Chicago mayoral election shows significant effects on the beliefs of voters of high, medium, and low political activity (Mulder, 1979). Unfortunately, most research in this area has been proprietary, and our understanding of the specific effects of political advertising is limited.

Political advertising is not the only persuasive tool available in this arena. One of the most effective tools, research indicates, is designed to listen to constituents by maximizing interpersonal contact with the public (Hesse, 1981). Professor Michael B. Hesse found that the most successful legislators are those who use information-gathering techniques to get a reading of their constituents' views. They avoid heavy reliance on one-way techniques, such as newsletters and direct mail, which provide little feedback.

Professors Ruth Ann Weaver and Theodore H. Glasser (1984) look at political communication from an organizational perspective. Based on a mail survey, they suggest that organizations need to understand legislator attitudes and needs in order to present their ideas effectively. Survey research, they contend, can be used in developing specific information programs for legislators.

International Public Relations

International public relations is one of the most rapidly growing areas of the profession, and one of the least understood. Michael Rowan (1986) of Strategic Information Research Corporation says, "This is where much of the future lies for the multi-nationals." He reports having just completed a public opinion study in China, where advertising from the West is now being permitted. "For $4,000 you can buy 60 seconds of TV time and reach 100 million viewers!" he adds.

Although there has been very little research on international public relations conducted in the public arena, one mail survey (Strenski, 1975) of the PR directors of the largest Fortune 500 companies reveals several problems facing international public relations. Heading the list is an urgent need to protect corporate interests abroad from rising nationalism, monetary fluctuations, and political upheavals. While some might contend American multinationals are getting what they deserve, the PR problems are still very real. Even the term *multinational* has taken on a negative meaning in foreign nations (and probably the United States, as well).

Research also shows that the management of international public affairs activities has been weak at best. A study (Blake & Toros, 1976) of how 38 U.S.-owned multinational corporations manage their international public affairs activities reveals that most do not "manage" this process. Furthermore, methods of identifying emerging social and political issues and incorporating them into planning and management functions are almost nonexistent. It is becoming increasingly important for multinational corporations to take an active, aggressive role in managing public affairs and communication efforts. This is clearly illustrated in the ongoing crisis in South Africa—where apartheid and U.S.-owned multinationals have hit a crossroads.

Professors Robert B. Albritton and Jarol B. Manheim (1983) recently found in a content analysis evidence of a successful international campaign to improve U.S. press coverage of a foreign nation. Their study shows that *New York Times*' coverage of Rhodesia improved significantly after that country hired a PR firm to advise it. News of violence was unaffected.

EVALUATION RESEARCH

Measuring the Effectiveness of Public Relations

A second broad area of research conducted to advance the profession focuses on measuring the effectiveness of PR efforts. Unfortunately, measuring the effectiveness of PR efforts has proved almost as elusive as finding the Holy Grail. The problem, it seems, is twofold. First, what do we measure? Second, how do we measure it? Professor Byron Reeves (1983) responds to the first question. He reports that a "full documentation of media effects (of a PR campaign) requires evidence from four sources":

(1) content of the message;
(2) audience exposure to the message;
(3) effects (results of exposure); and,
(4) conditional processes—situations when effects may or may not occur.

Evaluation researcher Carol H. Weiss (1972) identifies another important dimension of the measurement problem. She explains, "It is a common tendency" for PR practitioners to attempt evaluation of a program without ever specifying its purpose. Or, she adds, "If a statement of purpose was offered, it was often stated in terms of program activities, rather than program outcomes."

Examining data from a mail survey, Kirban (1983) also reveals an interesting insight into the psychology of evaluation. More than half the practitioners in a survey of members of the Chicago PRSA chapter expressed a "fear of being measured." Perhaps this reflects a fear of the unknown, or perhaps a fear that no effect will be found. Evaluation research is concerned with the "consequences" of the program. "What is the program trying to accomplish?" is the appropriate question. Unfortunately, many PR practitioners have often replied in fuzzy, global, and unmeasurable terms, such as "to improve goodwill."

This form of evaluation research is called *summative* (Scriven, 1967). It tells us whether a program has achieved its objectives, thus requiring that the program have clearly articulated, specific, and measurable objectives before the program is implemented. One of the important functions of summative evaluation is that it facilitates decision making. Summative research allows a program manager to decide whether to continue a program of action. It reaches the bottom line: go or no go.

Conducting summative research also requires measurements both before and after a campaign. Before-measures are needed to establish a baseline, a way of knowing where you are to begin with. After-measures are needed to assess whether the campaign has moved you to where you wanted to go. It is similar to taking a trip. To have a successful trip, you must know at least three things: (1) where you want to go, (2) where you are at to begin with, and (3) where you wind up. How you get there—your route on a trip or your strategy in a PR campaign—is also of critical importance, but is not part of a summative evaluation. Formative evaluation is the complement to summative evaluation. According to Weiss (1972), "Formative evaluation produces information that is fed back during development of curriculum to help improve it. It serves the needs of the developers." In this sense, formative evaluation provides diagnostic information on a traveler's route or a PR person's program strategy.

Formative research can take many forms, from seat-of-the-pants to scientific, quantitative measurement. Its usefulness lies in telling us how or whether to improve a PR program (or strategy). Formative research can tell us how to enhance the effectiveness of a program or how to eliminate the waste—trimming the fat.

Actual Evaluation Practices

More than 15 years ago, researcher Edward J. Robinson (1969) predicted that PR evaluation would move away from seat-of-the-pants approaches and toward "scientifically derived knowledge." He was suggesting that practitioners would no longer rely upon anecdotal, subjective measures of program success, such as feedback from personal contacts or winning awards. Rather, practitioners would begin to use more systematic measures of success, primarily social science methods such as survey research.

Has his prediction come true? This is the research question posed by Dozier (1984) in a recent study in San Diego, California. Dozier conducted a mail survey of 169 PR practitioners in the San Diego area to determine what styles they use in evaluating the success of their PR programs. He mailed questionnaires to 333 practitioners whose names had been obtained from the mailing lists of four major PR associations: the Public Relations Society of America, the International Association of Business Communicators, the Public Relations Club of San Diego, and Women in Communications. The 169 completed surveys represent a fairly good response rate for a mail survey (more than 50%).

Three Major Evaluation Styles

Dozier's survey reveals three major evaluation styles in common practice, at least among the practitioners in the San Diego area. These are (1) scientific impact evaluation, (2) seat-of-the-pants evaluation, and (3) scientific dissemination evaluation.

Scientific impact evaluation is the type of evaluation predicted by Robinson. It is program evaluation using primarily quantitative, social science methods of data collection to determine program impact. Samples of publics are drawn, surveys are taken, messages are tested, and public opinion poll data are monitored as part of scientific impact evaluation. Frequently, practitioners rely upon experimental or quasi-experimental research designs in which measures are taken both before and after a new program is implemented (e.g., Larson & Massetti-Miller, 1984). This design allows one to determine whether the program "caused" the observed change.

Seat-of-the-pants evaluation is the traditional approach used in public relations. It is typified by personalized, subjective evaluation in which anecdotal, casual observation or the judgment of the practitioner is used to estimate the effectiveness of a PR program. Practitioners using this approach are often more concerned with the PR process than with the actual outcomes of the campaign. They might obtain feedback through meetings with members of a key public, personal media contacts, or colleagues. They might often consider awards and other such peer recognition as an important measure of program success.

Scientific dissemination evaluation is another traditional method, one in which the focus is on the distribution of the message. It is often based upon a numeric analysis of clip files, a log of column inches or air time, the reach of the media used, or a content analysis of those clips (e.g., Marker, 1977). The focus in this approach is on the communication process. Impact is inferred from that process. For example, it is assumed that the more widely a message is disseminated, the greater its (potential) impact. While this is an intuitively attractive idea, an overwhelming amount of research shows that presentation of the message (i.e., dissemination) does not equal reception of the message. Moreover, there is no way to tell the manner in which the message is received or distorted.

A mail survey reported in *Public Relations Journal* (1982) shows similar uses of research among PR practitioners in the Chicago area. PRSA members report broad support for measuring the effectiveness of PR programs and the use of a variety of tools.

The *Public Relations Journal* survey also indicates several classes of evaluation research closely paralleling those found in Dozier's San Diego survey. The first two—opinion polls and surveys, and general feedback—are similar to Dozier's scientific impact evaluation. A third area, newspaper clips, is analogous to Dozier's "scientific dissemination" category. Finally, the Chicago survey's "subjective, internal meetings" category is very close to Dozier's "seat-of-the-pants" evaluation. Chicago respondents also feel that instituting systems for measurement will benefit both individual practitioners and programs, as well as the profession as a whole.

Of course, saying and doing are two different things (Hiebert & Devine, 1985; Lindenmann, 1980). Grunig elaborates (1983b):

> Lately, I have begun to feel more and more like the fundamentalist minister rallying against sin; the difference being that I have rallied for evaluation. Just as everyone is against sin, so most public relations people I talk to are for evaluation. People keep on sinning, however, and public relations people continue not to do evaluation research.

Professor James Bissland (1986) similarly found that while the amount of evaluation has increased, the quality of research has been slow to improve. He analyzed evaluation practices as reflected in Silver Anvil ("academy awards" of PR) winners, for 1981-1982 and 1984-1985. Bissland's analysis reveals that few programs satisfy Lazarsfeld's (1959) criteria for establishing causality: (1) time ordering—campaign before change, (2) correlation—a relationship between campaign objectives and observed changes, and (3) parsimoniousness—an economical design that rules out all alternative explanations (to be sure the PR campaign caused the change).

Mark P. McElreath (1977) of Arbitron Ratings suggests that the use and type of evaluation research is affected by environmental uncertainty and various organizational factors. To date, however, there has been little systematic research to test this proposition.

Evaluation Styles and Practitioner Roles

Dozier (1984) also looked at whether evaluation styles are related to the practitioner organizational roles developed by Broom (Broom & Smith, 1979). The two major roles Dozier studied are the communication technician and the communication manager. The communication technician specializes in communication activities, such as writing and placing press releases, editing the company newsletter, and writing speeches. These activities are often associated with entry-level positions.

The communication manager is a combined role, including problem solver, decision maker, and planner. Persons in this role tend to occupy high-ranking positions in the decision-making hierarchy and have high career aspirations. As high-ranking, top-paid executives, communication managers are expected to be innovators and to provide leadership. "In their comparison of 1979 and 1985 survey data from a panel of 208 PRSA members, Broom and Dozier (1986) found that increases in overall evaluation research activities were associated with increased participation in management decision making" (Broom, 1986).

Dozier's (1984) survey shows that communication technicians are likely not to use any style of evaluation. This is not surprising because as beginning professionals, evaluation activities are not emphasized. Their primary responsibility lies with the production and dissemination of the message. For the most part, if they do evaluate their efforts, they are equally likely to use any of the three styles. However, persons who specialize in media relations are likely to be heavy users of the scientific dissemination style of evaluation.

Meanwhile, communication managers are likely to rely upon the seat-of-the-pants approach and use the scientific impact evaluation style. Notably, however, the scientific impact evaluation style is more often used only as a supplement to the seat-of-the-pants approach. It is rarely used as a complete replacement for that more informal approach. Although this is a partial contradiction to Robinson's prediction, it is not entirely unexplainable. In Dozier's own words,

> The supplemental use of scientific evaluation is with the imperative that managers make decisions and act even when all information useful to decision making is not available.

Scientific research is not always completed in a timely fashion, nor is it always affordable. Thus, the communication manager must often rely on "gut instinct" and other informal methods of evaluation to determine whether a program is a success, or whether the decision is "go" or "no go."

Grunig (1983b) argues that we must establish a basic body of knowledge before practitioners can realistically and cost effectively use evaluation research. This basic research, he adds, must address these issues: (1) the nature of the public, (2) the effects different programs can have, and (3) the contribution public relations makes to organizational effectiveness.

BASIC RESEARCH ON PUBLIC RELATIONS

Basic research is designed to build a foundation of knowledge upon which the PR profession can rest. Much as doctors rely upon a basic body of knowledge to practice medicine, so too do practitioners of public relations need a knowledge base. Grunig (1983b) argues that basic research is the territory and responsibility of academic researchers. While he admits once having agreed with Bernays's view that practitioners are applied social scientists, he today feels this is an inaccurate statement. PR practitioners are "not scientists at all," although they should (few do) use theories and research on public relations and communication.

Referring to the medical analogy, Grunig goes on to suggest that academic researchers must build the basic body of knowledge about public relations, just as researchers in medical schools build a basic body of knowledge for practicing physicians.

The following discussion examines the basic body of knowledge that has developed through systematic research on public relations and persuasive communication in general.

The Classic Information-Processing Model

Although the field is evolving, the heart of public relations still lies in the arena of the public opinion process. Basic questions involve how public opinion is formed and how it is influenced by communication. The most well-known and well-researched model of the communication process and public opinion is the classic information-processing model of general attitude and behavior change. It is often called the Yale or Hovland Model because it was developed at Yale by Carl I. Hovland and his colleagues at Yale in the 1940s and 1950s (e.g., Hovland, Janis, & Kelley, 1953; Hovland, Lumsdaine, & Sheffield, 1949).

This model is based upon the idea that there are identifiable and distinct participants in the communication process, including the source, message, channel, and receiver. Further, the communication process can be facilitated by certain characteristics that these participants exhibit. For example, Hovland's research demonstrated that the credibility of a source influenced the persuasiveness of the message being delivered.

One of the most vocal supporters of this model has been Professor William J. McGuire (1969, 1972, 1981). He has developed a "persuasion matrix" as a way of understanding the complexities of the communication process, its inputs (i.e., participants), and outcomes.

In McGuire's matrix the first key "participant" in the communication process is the *source* of the message, for instance, a corporation, its spokesperson, or a public advocate such as Ralph Nader. The *message* itself is the next key actor, and it embraces both the substance and form of the communication (e.g., the topic and the complexity of the message). The *channel* refers to the medium through which the message will be distributed. In public relations, the channel is often a mass medium, such as television or newspaper, when reaching a large, external audience, and a specialized medium, such as a newsletter or annual report, when reaching a well-defined, internal audience. The *receiver* refers to the target audience—or public—that the source is trying to reach with its message. The final "participant" in this process is the destination. The *destination* refers to the type of outcome sought by the source. Key considerations here include whether the hoped-for outcome involves either a change in public opinion or a reinforcement of existing beliefs, either long-term or short-term effects, or behavioral versus knowledge versus attitudinal change.

McGuire (1981) identifies one dozen distinct outputs—or successive response steps—in his matrix. While we will not review all 12 here, we summarize them as follows. The first step is audience exposure to the message. This is followed by attention, liking, learning, agreement, remembering, and behavior. The basic premise of the persuasion matrix is that by manipulating the characteristics of the communication participants, one can facilitate movement through the persuasion steps. The matrix is used in planning public communication campaigns.

What Are the Findings?

Although there has been a vast and sometimes contradictory array of findings in this area, there are some conclusions we can draw (Anderson, 1986; Flay, 1981; Van Leuven, 1986). We will organize our discussion into the five main "input" areas identified by McGuire (1981).

Source

A communication is most persuasive when it comes from multiple sources of high credibility. Credibility is a multidimensional concept, including trustworthiness, expertise, and power. Power and trustworthiness are effective when the desired change is attitudinal or behavioral, expertise when the message is technical or complex, or if knowledge gain is the main goal (a dynamic source, such as a celebrity or highly attractive model, is useful if the audience has low involvement, and simple, straightforward, more personalized broadcast channels are employed).

Message persuasiveness is also aided by source-audience similarity (i.e., the source shares important audience characteristics, such as age, sex).

Message

Characteristics. A message generally is more effective when it is simple, because it is easier to understand, localize, and make personally relevant. More complex messages will result in more varied interpretations and decrease the likelihood of large numbers of people behaving in the desired manner.

A message should also target a specific issue and be repeated often (i.e., high frequency) and consistently (i.e., there are few contradictory or competing messages). Its effectiveness is also enhanced when it is presented in novel ways—in order to capture and maintain attention and increase the chance of arousing involvement.

Further, it is important that the message employ an appropriate appeal. Rational appeals are most effective when directed at cognitive outcomes because they are drive reducing. Emotional appeals are drive arousing and have greater effect on attitudinal outcomes by intensifying motivation. Fear appeals produce similar results. Negative appeals prompt more verbal responses to comply, but positive appeals are more effective for message retention and actual compliance.

Message effectiveness is also linked to the source. Perhaps most important, the message must have high compatibility with the source. Compatibility facilitates comprehension and attitude change, especially when the source classifies the message in the same way as members of the target audience. Familiarity with the source may inhibit cognitive effectiveness. Unknown sources lead to greater knowledge gain and comprehension since receivers have less reason to concentrate on the source, and more reason to remember arguments.

Scheduling. Professor Jim K. Van Leuven (1986) argues that there is at least one more set of important factors in designing a PR campaign message. This encompasses the coverage and timing of exposures to the message. While scheduling has long been of central importance in advertising, it has been often neglected in public relations. This is largely because PR campaigns have relied upon free air time and space, and thus had little control over message scheduling.

In determining reach and frequency goals, there are several important considerations. Perhaps most important, how many exposures are needed to produce the desired change? Advertising media planners call this "effective frequency" (Naples, 1979). It is a concept that incorporates both reach and frequency. Advertising research has generally shown that one exposure rarely produces any significant change. Instead, a range of 3-10 exposures during a one-month period is often needed. Similarly, there may be an exposure "threshold"—beyond which we will see significant change, and below which there will be no change. It is important to note that fewer exposures may be needed for news items. News items are often longer (in broadcast) and have a higher level of believability than do sponsored messages.

Van Leuven (1986) makes the following recommendations for message scheduling:

(1) reach is needed more than frequency when awareness is the goal;
(2) frequency is more important than reach in holding already converted publics; and
(3) frequency is needed to move an issue onto the agenda initially.

Channel

Van Leuven (1986) contends that there are at least three important aspects of channel selection: feedback opportunities, social cuing, and user control. The number and nature of feedback opportunities affect audience involvement and the way the message is perceived. Feedback is of increasing importance as the outcome moves from cognitive, to attitudinal, to behavioral. Feedback increases opportunities for repetition, clarification, elaboration, and even dialogue (i.e., interaction). Feedback is lowest with the mass media, highest with interpersonal channels, and moderate with interactive media.

Social cuing provides a "sense of actually being there." People will attend to and use messages that are amplified by supportive nonverbal and contextual cues. For example, the ability of film and television to use sight, sound, and motion tends to enhance the communication effectiveness of these channels, especially for affective messages. Social cuing can also be enhanced if mass media messages are supplemented by face-to-face communications.

Greater user control allows for more complex communications and leads to greater potential cognitive change. Print and interactive electronic media offer high user control.

Audience

The persuasiveness of a message can be increased when it arouses or is accompanied by a high level of personal involvement in the issue and is consistent with related attitude and value structures (i.e., members of the public care about the issue and are in fundamental agreement with the organization's basic position).

Similarly, a high level of social support or acceptance in the environment surrounding members of the public will enhance effectiveness. Since communication is part of the social environment, we prefer messages that are compatible with that environment. We can heighten this compatibility by localizing messages or associating the message with audience members' important personal values (O'Keefe & Reid-Nash, 1986). PSAs are more effective when dealing with topics around which social consensus already exists. One effective method for generating social support is by mobilizing or restructuring community resources.

Destination

Attitude and behavior change have been the traditional goals in public relations programs. In light of recent research, however, program goals have begun to shift to less powerful, intermediate stages in the information-processing model. For example, many programs today have as their immediate objective increasing awareness of an issue. Health communication specialist Brian R. Flay (1981) states, "It should be relatively easy to change people's awareness of certain issues as long as they can be exposed to information." Despite this, "few evaluations of mass media programs have bothered to measure exposure or awareness"—although many PR programs have probably failed because they did not even reach their target publics (Cartwright, 1949; Hyman & Sheatsley, 1947). As Flay (1981) sums up:

> Obviously, successful media campaigns need to be provided channels during popular listening and watching times. The failure of many public service announcements can probably be traced to their being aired during less popular programs at times when most of the target audience [is] not likely to be awake anyway.

Professor James E. Haefner (1976) supports this argument with evidence from an informational campaign using prime-time television spots. His audience survey revealed higher recall and comprehension rates for these prime-time spots than is usual for information campaigns.

Criticisms of the Classic Information-Processing View

As Flay (1981) points out, "The information-processing model generally assumes that changes in knowledge and beliefs will automatically lead to changes in attitudes, which will automatically lead to changes in behavior." Although much research from the 1940s to the early 1970s supported these views, a growing amount of recent research forces us to question these basic assumptions.

Hierarchies of Effects

A number of researchers (e.g., Ostrom, 1969; Ray, 1973) have demonstrated that the order of change is not limited to that presented in McGuire's matrix. Marketing researcher Michael L. Ray (1973), for example, suggests at least three basic orderings of the knowledge, attitude, and behavior elements. He calls these the "hierarchies of effects."

Flay (1981) notes that the "appropriateness of each (hierarchy) for a particular situation is most dependent upon the factors of involvement in the issue, and degree of differentiation of alternative behavioral responses." (One might view these as receiver and destination characteristics.)

When there is low audience involvement and little difference between the behavioral alternatives, Ray has shown that knowledge changes are likely to lead directly to behavior changes. In marketing this is well illustrated by typical consumer packaged-goods purchasing, such as the purchase of a tube of toothpaste or a roll of toilet paper. This ordering of effects is referred to as the "low-involvement" hierarchy (Krugman, 1965).

If audience involvement is high, but behavioral alternatives are few or almost indistinguishable, behavior change is likely to be followed by attitude change, and finally selective learning. Ray calls this the "dissonance-attribution" hierarchy for the following reasons. The attitude change occurs as a result of dissonance (Festinger, 1957)—uncertainty about the decision—or self-attributon—"if I choose this alternative, then it must be better (Flay, 1981)." The individual then selectively acquires knowledge in order to support the new behavior and attitude. Finally, when there are both high involvement in the issue and clear differences between the alternatives, the sequence of change is likely to be: knowledge, attitude, behavior. This is called the learning hierarchy, and assumes that people act in a very rational manner. First, they learn about an issue, then they evaluate their position on that issue in light of what they have learned, then they act in a manner consistent with their attitude and knowledge. This hierarchy also corresponds to McGuire's persuasion matrix.

Applications to Public Relations

How do the "hierarchies of effects" apply to PR situations? The learning hierarchy seems most appropriate for many PR situations. PR situations often involve highly differentiated behavioral choices, such as pledging $100 to the local public television station or spending it on luxury products advertised on a local commercial station. Further, involvement may be high when "the potential importance of the consequences of the behavioral choice is known" (Flay, 1981). A person making a donation to a local PBS station may feel that his or her pledge will help ensure quality programming. Of course, many people will give for a variety of "irrational" reasons—even persons highly involved. No single factor accounts for all the variation in human behavior.

The implications here for campaign planning are to design a message strategy that emphasizes information, not emotion. To explain why each person's pledge is needed, and to let each person see the direct benefits of his or her donation.

Frequently, key publics may not be highly involved in the issue. For example, a group of dairy organizations sponsor a "Dairy Day" each year in the State College, Pennsylvania, area. For most people in the region, the event does not hold great significance, nor do they feel a strong personal connection to the issue of dairy promotion. Of course, dairy farmers in the area are highly involved, but the key audience is the general public, milk drinkers, and ice cream connoisseurs. Thus, the low-involvement hierarchy may be most applicable in many public relations situations.

From a campaign planning point of view, this suggests the following strategy. The campaign should focus on highly repetitive, simple messages aimed at raising awareness of the issue, and its salient (i.e., short-term) "consequences." For example, a message promoting Dairy Day might emphasize the "free ice cream cone for all who attend," rather than the long-term health benefits of eating dairy products (i.e., calcium builds strong bones). In some cases, this strategy may lead not only to increased awareness of the issue but also to increased involvement. This consequence, however, is likely to be difficult to achieve and slow to occur. If it should occur, a second stage may be in order. This stage would focus more on messages designed to influence attitudes and behavior.

Finally, some PR situations may be highly involving, but the differences between the behavioral choices may be slight.

Hierarchies-of-effects research, as well as that by others (e.g., Grunig, 1986; Van Leuven, 1986), suggests a perhaps even more important reason for questioning the assumptions of the traditional information-processing model. This research indicates that a change in knowledge, attitudes, or behavior may not necessarily lead to any other change. Change is contingent upon certain situational factors. In the following discussion we will examine some of these key situational factors.

Situational Theory of Publics

Grunig (1976, 1978, 1983a) has developed an innovative situational theory of the communication process. His view is in contrast to the traditional "domino theory" of the communication process. In the domino theory, information is thought to lead to attitudes, which in turn lead to behavior. A growing body of research has demonstrated that this is often not the case (Stamm, 1972; Tichenor, Donohue, Olien, & Bowers, 1971). Furthermore, research suggests that demographic factors are often of little use in predicting or identifying individual attitudes or opinions. Instead, the relationship among knowledge, attitudes, and behavior is contingent upon a number of situational factors.

Grunig argues that there are four important factors in his situational theory of communication behaviors. They are (1) level of problem recognition, (2) level of constraint recognition, (3) presence of a referent criterion, and (4) level of involvement. Grunig argues that these factors determine the extent to and way in which a person communicates about an issue or organization. They also provide a way in which to identify publics.

Problem recognition refers to the extent to which a person sees that something is "missing or indeterminate in a situation so that he stops to think about the situation." It is based on John Dewey's (1938) idea that a person will not think or talk about a situation unless it is somehow a problem to him or her. Problem recognition thus increases the chances that a person will communicate about a situation.

Constraint recognition involves the extent to which a person sees his or her behavior as limited by environmental factors beyond his or her own control. Information that aids in decision making has little value to a person who has high constraint recognition. For example, a college student might recognize that apartheid in South Africa is a major problem. This student might also believe that there is very little or nothing that can be done to alleviate the situation. Therefore, he or she would place little value on information from a students-against-apartheid committee.

Grunig argues that these two factors—problem recognition and constraint recognition—can be combined to identify four types of perceived situations. Furthermore, Grunig's research indicates that these situations can help identify publics that demonstrate similar types of communication behaviors. He calls these: (1) problem-facing behavior (high problem recognition, low constraint recognition); (2) constrained behavior (high problem recognition, high constraint recognition); (3) routine behavior (low problem recognition, low constraint recognition); and (4) fatalistic behavior (low problem recognition, high constraint recognition). In each of these situations, members of a public may bring with them a referent criterion. A referent criterion is some piece of knowledge or experience a person brings with him or her from a previous situation. It acts largely as a decision rule for the person. If it works, the person will continue to use it in future situations. If it fails, the person will develop a new referent criterion—that is, a new solution. For example, experience might tell an employee that the best person to approach with a work-related problem is his or her direct supervisor. The employee will continue to do that indefinitely—unless that strategy begins to fail.

The fourth variable in Grunig's situational theory is the individual's level of involvement. *Involvement* refers to the extent to which a person perceives a connection between himself or herself and a situation. "The stronger the connection, the more probable it is that the person will communicate about it." For example, consider the recent epidemic of product-tampering episodes involving Tylenol capsules. Who is more likely to engage in some form of communication behavior regarding this issue—a person who regularly takes Tylenol capsules as a headache remedy or a person who regularly uses a tablet form of some other brand?

Level of involvement predicts not only whether a person will communicate about a situation but also the way in which he or she will do so. Grunig argues that we process information in two ways: actively and passively. Active information processing occurs when a person purposely seeks information or is "ready" to receive information about some situation. Active information processing is likely to take place when a person who has just swallowed two Tylenol capsules then hears a television reporter say that cyanide-laced Tylenol capsules have been discovered in a local pharmacy. This person is probably going to purposely seek out more information about the situation.

Passive information processing occurs when a person randomly receives messages or when he or she is using the media merely as a means of passing time. For instance, one might read a magazine while waiting for a hair appointment. Messages processed passively are less likely to be internalized or remembered.

Grunig's situational theory is quite complex and requires several readings before it is fully understood. Nevertheless, it is quite powerful in campaign planning and the identification of different types of publics. Grunig's research suggests that there are three basic types of publics that emerge in his situational theory. They are the latent public, the aware public, and the active public. The latent public exists when a group is in an "indeterminate situation but does not recognize the situation as problematic." When the group recognizes the problem, it becomes an aware public. Finally, when it organizes to discuss and do something about the problem, a group becomes an active public. This will typically occur when constraints are removed or when the group receives information that allows its members to act on their existing attitudes. This has been defined (Lemert, Mitzman, Seither, Cook, & Hackett, 1977) as mobilizing information.

In general, Grunig's ideas closely parallel those proposed by Dewey (1927). He said a public arises when a group of people "(1) faces a similar indeterminate situation, (2) recognizes what is indeterminate in that situation, and (3) organizes to do something about the problem." The key distinction between Dewey's concept and Grunig's is that Grunig views Dewey's three conditions as separate stages in the development of an active public. Referring to Grunig's situational theory, a public is likely to become active in the following situations: high involvement and high problem recognition. When involvement is high and problem recognition is low, a public is likely to become active only when a clear referent criterion is available. Otherwise, a public in an indeterminate situation is likely to remain latent.

Publics will tend to be either latent or aware when involvement is low, regardless of the level of problem recognition.

Research on Grunig's Situational Theory

In a survey of the effectiveness of a campaign against drunk driving, Grunig and Daniel Ipes (1983) found evidence that a public information campaign must do more than present information. It must show people how they can remove constraints to their personally doing something about the problem. The researchers also found that while problem recognition can raise involvement, it has no effect on constraint recognition or removal.

Grunig (1983c) has also found this situational theory useful in identifying reporter publics. In a survey of Washington journalists, he distinguishes reporter publics on the basis of several situational factors, including their personal interest in environmental issues, perceived reader interest in environmental issues, and certain institutional factors. While Grunig's own research tends to confirm and refine his situational theory, how has it fared when tested by other scholars? So far, it has stood up well.

Communications graduate student Ronald Anderson (1986) supports these findings through his analysis of a series of experimental campaigns against drunk driving. He concludes that removing behavioral constraints—such as psychological barriers to action—will increase the odds of producing behavior change in mass media campaigns. Hyman and Sheatsley (1947) anticipated these ideas in their seminal study on why information campaigns fail.

Professor Larissa S. Grunig (1985) recently looked at the results of a mail survey of employees in a university-based research and development program. The results confirm that the communication behaviors and activity levels are based upon each employee's situation. More specifically, the information sought by employees is of a situational nature. In this fashion, Grunig was able to identify three employee types: (1) information seekers, (2) selective information processors, and (3) nonselective information processors. Employee communicators can use this situational framework to analyze the information needs of employees. For example, information seekers tended to want more research and administrative content in their internal publications.

Further Applications of the Situational Theory

Other research has examined the relationship between communication situations and certain cognitive strategies. Consider, the cognitive strategies of hedging and wedging identified by Professors Keith R. Stamm and Grunig (1977; Grunig & Stamm, 1979). Hedging is a cognitive strategy in which a person holds two or more conflicting views on a solution to a problem. It is analogous to hedging a bet at a racetrack. One might bet on a long shot at the Kentucky Derby, but hedge his or her bet with $2 on the favorite. It increases the chances of being a winner.

Research on public relations indicates that a hedging strategy is especially likely to be used when the person lacks a referent criterion or has little prior information. Wedging is a cognitive strategy of firmly holding one position. It is similar to driving a wedge under a door to firmly hold it open. Research shows that on many environmental issues, highly involved persons are likely to use a wedging strategy.

INTROSPECTIVE RESEARCH

The third broad class of PR research, in addition to basic and applied research, is introspective. It is research looking inward at the field of public relations. There are several major research questions asked in this body of research. First, there is sociological research on roles and gender differences in PR practice. This also includes descriptive research looking at public relations as a field of employment—what are the salaries, job titles, and so on. Second, there is research looking at professionalism in the field. This includes research on professional associations in public relations, social responsibility, and licensing. Finally, there is a large amount of research dealing with the nature of PR education at the college or university level.

Sociological Research: Roles and Gender in Public Relations

Glen M. Broom, a PR professor at San Diego State University, has been a pioneer in roles research in public relations. In the 1970s, Broom began systematically studying the different kinds of roles in which PR practitioners might operate. His research, based on a laboratory experiment testing practitioners' impact on client perceptions, led him to conceptualize four roles frequently played by practitioners (Broom, 1982; Broom & Smith, 1979). They are the communication technician, the expert-prescriber, the communication facilitator, and the problem-solving process facilitator. According to Broom's research, many practitioners often operate as sellers of services, *communication technicians*. A typical scenario might be as follows. After working for 12 years as a newspaper reporter, a woman decides to enter the field of public relations—in which the salaries are often somewhat higher. As a reporter, she has been in frequent contact with PR people and knows that much of their time is spent dealing with the media. Her experience as a reporter makes her an expert in media relations: She knows how to get a story in the paper. She is quickly hired by a local firm to handle their media relations. Her primary responsibilities are to write press releases for her company, and to handle media inquiries. She is a communication technician. Her role in that company does not involve policy or decision making.

The *expert-prescriber* role is quite different from that of the communication technician. Broom argues that it is somewhat analogous to that of a doctor-patient relationship. Like most people, I usually go to the doctor when there is something wrong. I think I've broken something, I've got the flu, or have some other ailment. I go to the doctor because she is an expert in health care. Her knowledge about the human body is far greater than mine—at least that is what I believe. I trust her judgment. She will diagnose the problem, give me a prescription, and, within a short period of time, I will be fine—usually.

So it is with the expert-prescriber role in public relations. The PR practitioner is consulted when a problem arises. A crisis arises—perhaps a major investor is poised to make an unfriendly takeover attempt of our corporation, including a purchase offer to all present stockholders. Uncertain as to our next move, we call a PR consultant in New York. As an expert in financial relations, she recommends making an immediate counteroffer to our stockholders, as well as a series of other strong steps. We follow this advice, and eventually avoid the takeover attempt.

Unfortunately, not all scenarios work out as happily as this one. The expert-prescriber role is a reactive one—it follows the traditional PR technique of putting out fires, rather than preventing them. As in the doctor-patient scenario played out earlier, the PR expert often merely treats symptoms, while the real problem goes undetected. Ultimately, this may lead to disaster.

Another key role identified in Broom's survey is that of the *communication facilitator*. Public relations in this role is characterized by the balanced two-way flow of information between an organization and its publics. The responsibility of the PR practitioner is both to disseminate the company's message and to obtain feedback from its important audiences. In this role, the goal is often to increase mutual understanding between the involved groups; to help each side see the other's point of view. While the communication-facilitator role may not offer a solution to all crisis situations, it can help build healthy long-term relationships.

Finally, there is the *problem-solving process facilitator*. This role, according to most research, is just beginning to emerge in the field. In it the PR practitioner serves a management function. She is a decision-maker, helping to identify problems and opportunities, recommending and implementing courses of action. Research serves an important function in this role, helping to identify problems, elicit feedback from publics, and evaluate program success.

Based on an examination of survey data from a panel of 208 PRSA members, Broom and Dozier (1986) provide current information on how salaries relate to these roles. Heading the list is the expert-prescriber, who earns an average of $67,700, followed by the problem-solving process facilitator at $54,300, the communication-process facilitator at $44,600, and the communication technician at $37,800.

These roles also have been found to have an impact on client perceptions. The pioneering study by Broom and practitioner George D. Smith (1979) reveals high client ratings of the problem-solving process facilitator role. Meanwhile, clients tend to view communication facilitators as "yes-sayers" and do-nothings.

More recent investigations indicate that practitioners usually operate in a combination of roles. In 1982 Broom reported the results of a survey of PRSA members designed to compare male and female roles in public relations. From the results, Broom determined that practitioners see themselves in only two broad roles—communication technician and some combination of the other three models.

Broom and Dozier's (1986) examination of panel data from 1979 to 1985 shows that the planning-management function of public relations is becoming increasingly important. This survey of 208 practitioners from the national PRSA roster identified the four following roles: (1) communication manager, (2) communication technician, (3) communication liaison, and (4) media relations specialist. The communication manager is a policymaker. He or she engages in systematic planning and often operates in an expert-prescriber or problem-solving process facilitator mode. The communication technician is often from the ranks of journalism and produces the organization's communication products, such as newsletters, press releases, and annual reports. He or she is not involved in policy-making. The communication liaison is not a policy-maker, either, serving primarily as a facilitator of two-way communication. The media relations specialist seeks to place messages in the media and deals with media representatives.

Although most practitioners occasionally serve in each of the four roles, there tends to be one dominant role (Acharya, 1985; Culbertson, 1985). According to Broom and Dozier (1986), the major roles are the communication manager and the communication technician. The communication liaison and media relations specialist tend to be minor roles in public relations.

Feminization of Public Relations

Women have played a very important part in the development of public relations. As Professor Marjorie K. Nadler (1986) points out, public relations is a field that is rapidly increasing its percentage of women, and current data suggest the trend is likely to expand even further. Practitioner Bill Cantor (1984), president of the Cantor

Concern, Inc., reports that women hold more than half (55%) of the jobs in public relations, and the percentage is growing. Further, the Public Relations Student Society of America (PRSSA) reports that the vast majority (79%) of its members were female in 1984-1985, while just a third (35%) were so in 1970-1971. A *Public Relations Reporter* survey (1985) shows that more than three-quarters of the entrants to the PR field between the ages of 25 and 29 are female.

Janet Diedrichs, a PRSA member in Chicago, sums up (Joseph, 1985-1986), "I think that there is a feminization of public relations. I think that it is not clear what the impact of that will be."

Barbara Finch, St. Joseph's Hospital, Kirkwood, Missouri, suggests an answer, "The prestige of the profession goes down, salaries plummet, and the entire profession suffers." Many in a recent mail survey (Joseph, 1985-1986) disagree, arguing that more women may improve the image of the field. One question that most agree on is will management accept women, or treat them as second-class citizens?

The role of women, however, has been somewhat different than that of men, as a recent study by Broom (1982) demonstrates. His practitioner survey shows that men tend to see themselves in the expert-prescriber role, while women see themselves in the communication technician role.

There are a number of other significant differences between male and female practitioners, as well. A survey of 1980 PR graduates (Teahan, 1982) shows a large salary differential—among students receiving a B.A., females had an average starting salary of $11,990, while males had $13,717. Among those receiving an M.A., females received $13,914, while males earned $15,600. Surveys conducted in the last two years (Beyer, 1986; Theus, 1985) confirm these salary differences still exist—although they are shrinking. An insert poll of *Public Relations Journal* readers reveals that women's salaries increased about 10% from 1984, while men's increased only 9% (Beyer, 1985). Women, however, tend to be concentrated in the lower salary brackets. Of those earning less than $35,000, 70% are female—85% of those earning more than $65,000 are male.

Researcher Kathryn T. Theus's (1985) mail survey also shows that males are twice as likely as females to be extremely satisfied with their salaries, jobs, and chances for career advancement. On the other hand, both men and women report higher salaries in PR fields than their counterparts in news-related positions (Nayman, McKee, & Lattimore, 1977).

Women in public relations also express some other important attitudinal differences (Selnow & Wilson, 1985; Turk, 1986). Females express anxiety over successful entry into a formerly male-dominated career. Women place greater emphasis than men on creativity, interpersonal interaction, societal values, and writing skills.

The factors leading to these gender differences are many and complex (Cline et al., 1986; Gorney, 1975; Turk, 1986). To a certain degree, women tend to occupy lower, entry-level positions—and thus serve as communication technicians—because they are more likely to be new to the field. Furthermore, college-level PR education has been a somewhat different experience for women than for men. For example, there have been fewer female role models. Similarly, women more than men have been encouraged to view public relations as a communication function rather than a management function. This too is due largely to educational and socialization differences between men and women. Finally, sexist attitudes and discriminatory practices still exist in the professional world (as well as in the academic world).

Turk (1986) perhaps summed it up best when she concluded, "Women, who never were taught the rules of the playing field to begin with, must play an aggressive game of catch-up to reach parity with their male counterparts in the career fields of public relations and business communications. Some women do appear to have gotten that message and are learning what men have known for a long time: upward mobility isn't just achieved on merit, it needs to be helped along by a mentor or network."

A recent study of female practitioners in Canada (Scrimger, 1985) shows many of the same findings as the previous American investigations. While women have increased greatly in numbers, they still have lower salaries, less authority, and fewer management positions; and only a few feel they can exert influence on policy-making in their organization.

Working in Public Relations

We are in the midst of an information revolution. According to the U.S. Census, more than half the working population is employed in the "service sector." The PR profession has been a major part of this continuing trend.

Based upon a recent study of U.S. Census data, Department of Labor statistics, organizational directories, and occupational research, Professor Robert Kendall (1984b) projects "phenomenal" growth for the PR industry. He predicts that by the end of the century, public relations will account for one million jobs. This represents more than a tripling of the number of PR jobs in the next 15 years. Considering all related PR services (i.e., various tools and techniques), the total number of PR-related positions could reach three million by the year 2000.

It remains to be seen how this growth will affect the salary structure in public relations, but to date, most surveys reveal a rather lucrative field of employment.

One survey (Morrissey, 1978) that is already several years old reveals an average salary of $26,000, and an average age of 45 among all PR practitioners. The salaries are undoubtedly higher today, with more practitioners occupying decision-making positions. Practitioner Matthew W. Miller (1982) reports a median salary of $59,300 for top corporate PR executives of Fortune 500 companies.

A Towers, Perrin, Forster and Crosby, Inc. survey (1984) also reveals above- average salaries in the not-for-profit industry. Based on a review of 23 executive positions in 178 not-for-profit organizations, this mail survey indicates a base salary increase of 7.9% from 1982-1983. Salaries range from $30,000 for those in information services, to $35,000 for those in editorial services, to $47,400 for the top PR positions. These positions also have numerous supplemental benefits, including life insurance, professional club and association membership, and parking! A *Public Relations Journal* (Lehrman, 1985a) survey shows that the most rapidly rising PR salaries are in the utilities, industrial, and consumer products fields. Close behind are PR firms and other consulting areas. Professors Robert L. Bishop and Allen M. Bosworth (1986) report similar statistics from a survey of 235 practitioners. They found that the overwhelming majority of the private enterprise (76%) and government (83%) practitioners have an income greater than $30,000. Less than half of those in entertainment or "altruistic" (e.g., nonprofit, religious) fields earn more than $30,000 annually. Practitioners in business-oriented sectors are given more prestige by fellow practitioners, as well, according to the Bishop and Bosworth study.

What is needed to land a position in public relations? Much research indicates the most important qualities are communication skills, especially good writing (Haskins, 1981; Kendall & Anderson, 1985-1986; Lumby, 1980; Proctor, 1983; Wilcox, 1979). Experience in any of the professional communication areas is also an asset, especially in career advancement. An understanding of economics and business, as well as the social sciences, is increasingly important.

Professionalism

Professionalism represents the second broad area of introspective public relations research. Much of the research in this area deals with the nature and membership of professional PR associations, especially the accrediting body, PRSA, one of two leading national organizations in the field. The International Business Communicators Association (IABC) is the other. One recent study (Rada, 1983) reveals that corporate and agency practitioner interest in PRSA is not very high. This and other studies suggest that professional associations need to improve their marketing efforts toward the established professional, whose involvement is needed by local chapters and younger professionals (Gilsdorf & Vawter, 1983).

Research also underscores the importance of educators' involvement in professional PR associations. According to a survey by Professors David E. Clavier and Donald K. Wright (1982), educators overwhelmingly report that it is very important for PR educators to belong to professional associations. More than half (54%) say it is important for faculty (advisors) to belong to the parent professional society.

Accreditation by PRSA and its relationship to perceived professionalism has also been studied. A mail survey by Wright (1981) shows that accredited practitioners (APR) are ranked as being more professional—but the level of APR is still low. Accreditation is often seen as a prerequisite to the complete public acceptance of public relations as a profession. Some have also contended that we must go so far as to have governmental licensing of PR practitioners. This position is perhaps most vocally advocated by Bernays (1986), who heads a committee studying the professionalism and licensing of PR practitioners, called, The Public Relations Practitioners for Licensing and Registration (PRPLR). He says licensing "is the only way for PR to become a profession." This is substantiated by a decision of the Appellate Division of the New York Supreme Court. The decision states: "A profession is not a business. It is distinguished by the requirements of extensive formal training and learning, admission to practice by a qualifying licensure." Bernays also reports that the committee's research has identified a list of 132 different titles used to refer to "public relations," which reflects the fragmented nature of the field of public relations, Bernays argues.

He goes on to say, "Initial public reaction has been encouraging. I have received letters from outstanding practitioners approving our effort." He adds that numerous publications have published articles supporting his committee's work. Bernays concludes, "The momentum of public opinion will go on to bring about the licensing and registration I had envisioned in my book *Crystallizing Public Opinion* in 1923 and which I have fought for in the interests of public relations and the public for five decades."

While Bernays, who first proposed licensing of PR practitioners in 1925, is optimistic, most practitioners, according to recent research, are opposed to governmental licensing. Kalupa and C. Gay Seivers (1986) conducted a mail survey of 400 practitioners from the PRSA and IABC rosters to assess attitudes toward licensing. "Only 2.9 percent of the practitioner respondents agreed with the key statement: Public relations practitioners should be licensed by the government. None of the respondents strongly agreed." The vast majority (86.5%) disagreed. Educator respondents are similarly opposed to government licensing. Most practitioners and educators see government licensing as a great potential infringement on their first amendment rights (Kalupa & Seivers, 1986; Tennant, 1978). They also feel that if licensing becomes mandatory, it should be done at the state government level (Tennant, 1978). Most practitioners see certification as a much more acceptable alternative to licensing. About half feel that certification is "essential to the professional development of the field."

Social Responsibility

Are PR practitioners socially responsible in the performance of their communication tasks? Many critics claim they are not. Consider the term *flack* (from writer Henry James's fictional character, George Flack), a rather unflattering slang term for press agent or PR practitioner often used by journalists.

Mail surveys of practitioners, however, suggest that as a whole, they have a moderate to high level of morality on legal, economic, and religious grounds and a concern for the public interest (Ryan & Martinson, 1985; Wright, 1985). Older practitioners, Wright reports, tend to have a stricter code of ethics than younger practitioners. Professors Michael Ryan and David L. Martinson (1984), in a survey of practitioners, found that "subjectivism" or individual relativism is the prevailing moral-ethical theory. Subjectivism theory is one of accountability—it is based on the belief that each of us is responsible for our own actions. According to Ryan and Martinson, many practitioners believe they are accountable to "an authority higher" than the corporation. For most practitioners, professionalism does not equal social responsibility. It is much more than that, including ethical values (Ryan & Martinson, 1984) and a basic body of knowledge upon which the field is based. Frustrations are felt by practitioners, however, because their jobs do not provide the level of professionalism and social responsibility they expect

(Wright, 1979). They are also concerned because public relations is without a comprehensive self-governing program and an enforceable code of ethics. Some research has also linked professionalism and effective communication between PR practitioners and management (Stephens, 1981; Wright, 1976). A mail survey by Wright (1983) reveals only minimal differences among men and women concerning social responsibility.

Public Relations Education

Studies of PR education constitute the third major area of introspective research. Most studies have focused on how public relations is taught, what students learn about public relations, and to what extent students are being prepared for the future needs of the profession. A series of recent investigations reveals that there is a trend away from "journalism omnipresence" in PR sequences and courses toward stronger and more expansive PR programs—although most PR educators received their B.A.s in journalism (Kendall & Anderson, 1985-1986). Using evidence from mail surveys, Professors Albert Walker and Paul V. Peterson (*Public Relations Journal,* 1982) conclude that PR programs are increasingly using an interdisciplinary approach, with "currents flowing from business, management and industry. There is also much cross-fertilization between advertising and public relations." Most studies in this area have confirmed the continuing growth of student demand for PR education (Walker, 1976, 1982). A number of practitioners, however, have lamented the relatively small number of accredited PR programs (Kalupa & Bateman, 1980).

The importance of writing and other communication skills in a PR curriculum is confirmed by a survey conducted for the Committee on Undergraduate PR Education under the co-chairmanship of Illinois Bell's Betsy Ann Plank and educator William P. Ehling (Kendall & Anderson, 1985-1986). The researchers analyzed responses from 544 leading PR educators responding to a mail questionnaire. Rating the importance of 110 elements commonly involved in a PR curriculum, respondents identified marketing, print communication processes, publicity and media relations, journalism skills, and goal setting as most important in a PR education.

Surveys also indicate that while writing and other communication skills still make up the most important area of education, theory, techniques, and case studies of public relations are rated of only slightly less importance by practitioners and educators (Baxter, 1985; Burger,

1981; Center, 1977; Gitter, 1981; Kalupa & Allen, 1982; Kendall & Anderson, 1985-1986; Ris, 1977; Stone, 1976; Walker, 1984; Wright, 1982).

One significant trend of the past 10 years has been an increase in the use of internships (Kendall, 1980), involvement in the Public Relations Student Society of America (PRSSA), Professional-Student mentoring, and other mechanisms for increased communication between the professional and academic communities, as in the form of case studies (Broom, Ferguson-DeThorne, & Ruksza, 1980).

Graduate education in public relations is another important area of research concern. A survey of 200 PRSA members reveals that practitioners feel the M.B.A. degree provides the best advanced education for public relations (Baxter, 1985). This reflects the growing demand for better-trained decision makers and managers in public relations. Practitioner Engelina Jaspers and Professor A. George Gitter (1982) conducted a mail survey of all accredited PR master's degree programs. This represents a total of 14 schools—seven accredited M.B.A. and seven accredited communications programs. The research question: Are PR graduate students learning what they should? The answer: not really. The survey reveals that there is only a 20% overlap between the M.B.A. and communications programs. Most of the areas of study are dissimilar. The only similarity is that both require students to study quantitative research methods. The M.B.A. programs tend to be somewhat technical in nature, emphasizing things such as account principles, finance, and production-operations management. While such programs do include the study of management science and human resource management, Jaspers and Gitter conclude there is no emphasis on the basic principles of management and public relations. The communications programs also have no emphasis on management, although they do include the foundations of public relations. While the communications programs place great emphasis on communication theory and PR principles, they lack any focus on oral communications, according to Jaspers and Gitter.

The future of PR education to a large degree rests on the shoulders of the teachers. What does research tell us about the teachers of public relations? One survey (Johnson & Rabin, 1977) suggests that while most college instructors are qualified to teach the basic courses, they are not contributing heavily to the body of knowledge in public relations. This has begun to change in the 1980s, but there is still a long way to go. Many teachers also have some recent professional experience to rely upon in skills courses, but they are not in a position to keep their knowledge current. Salaries are also not commensurate with the expenses that faculty members face (Kendall, 1984a).

Similarly, although course offerings in public relations have doubled in the past 10 years, the number of faculty has not increased proportionately (Kendall, 1984a). PR faculty are generally in the minority in their departments—often a 6:1 ratio. The result is an overly heavy teaching load for most PR teachers.

Another major concern in higher education and public relations is the image of public relations in mass communication texts. A recent content analysis reveals several problems in these texts (Cline, 1982). First, a general confusion exists in most texts about the tasks of advertising and public relations. Second, there is a consistent lack of consistent historical backgrounding. Third, there is what Cline (1982) calls "an insidious bias" that characterizes PR practitioners as "journalists who have sold out."

Of course, mass communication texts are not alone in their inadequate representation of public relations. A content analysis of basic PR texts reveals a significant problem in the handling of "honesty" in PR communication. Professor Hugh M. Culbertson contends the (1983) texts tend to speak in "absolutist" tones—that is, it's either honest or a lie. Meanwhile, conventional wisdom suggests a more "situationist" view on the part of young professionals. As a result, PR students fail to get a well-rounded view of the issues related to honesty in communication.

SUMMARY

This chapter has examined the major findings of three themes of research: applied, basic, and introspective. Findings from applied research tell us much about PR strategy and evaluation. Specifically, we have identified key characteristics of various PR tools and techniques. For example, research indicates that perceived distance and economic importance may be at least as important as physical proximity in determining the newsworthiness of a press release. Research also tells us that there are two important forms of evaluation in public relations: formative and summative. Formative is used in program development, while summative tells about program effectiveness or success. Other studies have revealed that there are three main evaluation styles employed in the field: seat-of-the-pants, scientific dissemination, and scientific impact evaluation. Basic research tells us much about the communication processes underlying the field of public relations. An extensive body of research supports the classic information-processing model of general attitude change. Meanwhile, recent research by Grunig and others indicates that a more situational view is often effective in defining publics. Introspective research offers insights into the sociology and professionalism of public relations. Studies indicate that practition- ers tend to operate in either of two major roles: communication technician or communication manager. Other investigations have explored the increasing feminization of the field. Finally, research on professionalism indicates that most practitioners are opposed to governmental licensing of the practice. In the area of social responsibil- ity, studies suggest that practitioners often subscribe to "subjectivism theory"—that we are each accountable for our own actions.

4

BEYOND COMMON SENSE

Systematic scholarly information can tell us many things that commonsense impressions alone cannot—the effect of PR activities on media content or why some traditional PR goals must be questioned.

Although there has been relatively little research dealing specifically with PR concepts and theory, there has been a considerable amount of communications research that has important implications for the field of public relations. One such area deals with the cumulative findings of research on the cognitive effects of the media.

FINDINGS FROM COMMUNICATION RESEARCH

Telling People What to Think (about)

For more than 50 years, PR people have been trying to tell people what to think. We call this *persuasion*. One of their main tools has been the mass media—newspapers, television, radio. Social scientists studying the media have found consistent evidence that the media, however, rarely change attitudes and behavior, especially among adults. Numerous studies from the 1940s on have shown that the media are more often conduits for information or forms of home entertainment than mass persuaders. Broadcast researcher Joseph T. Klapper's (1960) "law of minimal consequences" probably best sums up this body of research (McCombs, 1977). It suggests that the media's power is somewhat limited and "functions through a nexus of mediating factors." Often effects are greatest in the area of knowledge acquisition.

For public relations, the implication of this strong body of research is that persuasion may be an unrealistic goal for mass media campaigns. Bernays insightfully suggested this when he said his PR efforts were designed only to help "people go where they want to be lead" (Moyers, 1983).

The Agenda-Setting Function of the Media

If the media rarely persuade, what can they do? The answer was provided by political scientist Bernard C. Cohen in *The Press and Foreign Policy* (1963): "The press may not be successful much of the time in telling people what to think, but it is stunningly successful in telling its readers what to think about." This passage has come to be known as "the agenda-setting function" of the mass media. It has important implications for public relations.

The agenda-setting function of the media suggests a much more realistic set of goals for PR media campaigns. Rather than trying to influence personal attitudes and feelings directly, media campaigns will have much greater success in getting people to think about certain issues or organizations. PR campaigns utilizing the media will find it more feasible to raise the saliency or awareness of an issue than to shape public opinion about that issue. Professor Harold Mendelsohn stresses this point in his 1973 article, "Some Reasons Why Information Campaigns Can Succeed." He contends that media-based campaigns can succeed if their primary goal is to produce change in awareness, knowledge, or perception, rather than in behavior. One must assume, he says, that most of the members of the audience have little interest in what is being communicated. These are the psychological barriers first cited by Hyman and Sheatsley (1947) in their classic article, "Some Reasons Why Information Campaigns Fail." Thus, the primary goal of a media campaign must be to raise the public's level of interest in the issue.

Why is this an important goal for public relations? Respected scholar Walter Lippmann provides the answer in the opening chapter of his classic, *Public Opinion* (1921), "The World Outside and the Pictures in Our Heads." Lippmann argues convincingly in this chapter that behaviors are responses to and based upon pictures in our heads as shaped by mass media coverage of the outside world. This is especially true for things we often cannot experience directly, such as a political convention, a war in the Middle East, or a summit between President Reagan and Soviet leader Gorbachev.

Systematic Testing of the Agenda-Setting Function

Maxwell McCombs (McCombs, 1974, 1977; McCombs & Shulte, 1975) has been one of the leading scholars studying the agenda-setting function of the media. He has teamed up with Donald Shaw (e.g., Shaw & McCombs, 1977) on a number of occasions to study this important media effect. Their findings, along with those of others (Benton & Frazier, 1976; Cohen, 1975; Sobel, 1982), suggest four key areas of concern in agenda-setting research:

(1) the nature of the public agenda
(2) the nature of the mass media agenda
(3) the time lag between the appearance of an issue in the media agenda and the public agenda; and,
(4) the nature of the relationship between the mass media and public agendas

The Public Agenda. In *The Making of the President 1972* (1973), Pulitzer Prize winner Theodore H. White says, "It [the press] sets the agenda of public discussion; and . . . determines what people will talk and think about." White's insightful comment suggests at least two ways of looking at the public agenda: what people think about and what they talk about. These reflect what McCombs (1977) calls the intrapersonal and interpersonal public agendas.

The *intrapersonal agenda* refers to the set of issues that a person considers important to him- or herself. They are the issues that he or she thinks about and values highly. One study shows that exposure to crime news is a better predictor of issue salience than is personal experience with crime. This suggests a clear intrapersonal agenda-setting effect of the media.

The *interpersonal agenda* refers to the set of issues that a person shares with another, through discussion or some other communication. While these issues may overlap with those on the intrapersonal agenda, there is by no means a perfect match. For example, students at many American universities spend a lot of time talking about the issue of their university's divestment of financial investments in South Africa. For a large number of those students, however, the issue may not take on great personal importance. Rather, they may talk about it because students have set up a "shantytown" on campus or are boycotting all university businesses, such as is the case at the main campus of the Pennsylvania State University. One study (Atwood, Sohn, & Sohn, 1978) shows that newspaper coverage is most likely to influence the interpersonal agenda when nonlocal issues are involved.

Research suggests that there is at least one more type of public agenda, which McCombs (1977) calls the community agenda. This agenda reflects the set of issues of importance at the community level. One might obtain a sense of this agenda by examining the local government's budget allocations; those items with greater financial allocations are higher on the community agenda. Media agenda-setting effects on the "community" agenda are also reflected in a study by academics Sheldon Gilberg, Chaim Eyal, McCombs, and David Nicholas (1980). Their content analysis of President Carter's state of the union address, delivered January 18, 1978, and news media coverage surrounding it yields evidence that the media may have set the agenda for the message delivered by the president.

The Mass Media Agenda. Determining the media agenda is normally based on a systematic content analysis. The major issue of concern is what factors best reflect the media agenda? Is the amount of time or space allocated to a certain issue the best reflector of importance on the media agenda? How does placement come into play? How much weight should be assigned to stories run on the front page of the local newspaper or first in the nightly newscast? What other factors affect the prominence of a story? Headline size? Photos or graphics?

A related issue involves the nature of the media themselves. Which media should we consider? Should we consider a mix of different media? Do different media have different effects on the public agendas?

To date, the favorite media for agenda-setting research have been television and newspapers (McCombs, 1977). Some studies have examined these media separately, and some have looked at them in tandem. These media are the dominant ones for news, and most agenda-setting research has focused on political issues (e.g., Allen & Weber, 1983; Nord, 1981; Williams, Shapiro, & Cutbrith, 1983). Recently, a number of studies have examined the agenda-setting process outside the political arena. For example, health researcher Judith L. Sobel (1982) studied agenda setting in the area of heart health, and Professor Ardyth B. Sohn (1978) looked at agenda setting in the economic realm. Studies in these areas also have focused on the media of newspapers and television.

Shaw and McCombs (1977) studied both media in an agenda-setting investigation of the 1972 presidential election. They found that the role of the two media in agenda setting is quite different. Newspapers tend to be quite important in affecting the interpersonal and intrapersonal public agendas on political issues. Meanwhile, television seems to play a secondary role. Newspapers tend to be the "prime movers," in the sense that they determine what items will make it onto the agenda. Television acts more as a "spotlight," primarily serving to reorder the top few items on this agenda. Radio and cable television have also demonstrated a similar effect in an off-election year (Williams & Larson, 1977).

Time Lag. Time is an important issue in all research on public relations. How long does it take to produce the desired effect or change?

This is an especially important issue in research on agenda setting.

Overall, the research to date suggests a time lag of roughly two to six months (McCombs, 1977; McCombs & Shulte, 1975; Stone & McCombs, 1981). It is important to remember that this is only an average, and that the time lag between the media and public agendas may be almost nonexistent in some situations, and more than a year in others. Take for example the recent disaster of the U.S. Space Shuttle Challenger. Almost overnight people were considering the issue of whether to continue the space program, and in what form. This was true from the community agenda level on down to the intrapersonal level. (The community agenda is reflected in the federal government's investigation of NASA.)

In contrast, an issue such as Watergate can take a very long time to develop, with a time lag of many months. Shaw and McCombs' research on the 1972 presidential election likewise shows a rather lengthy time lag between the media and public agendas. Specifically, the public agenda in the fall of 1972 reflects the media agenda from the preceding spring and summer.

In general, an issue must remain on the media agenda for a long time for it to reach the public agenda. Furthermore, for it to remain on the media agenda for that long, the issue must have considerable newsworthiness. These are two of the major obstacles facing the PR person planning a media campaign.

The Nature of the Relationship. How does the media agenda affect the public agenda? Professors Gladys Engel Lang and Kurt Lang offer a clear rationale in *The Battle for Public Opinion* (Lang & Lang, 1983). "Prominence gives a news item the visibility that facilitates one's attention. Continuity allows for the kind of reiteration and development of news angles that help to fix the basic elements of the story in one's mind. Both are conducive to the emergence of an issue."

Research suggests that there are at least three kinds of media agenda-setting effects. First, media coverage can build awareness of an issue. For example, consumer product tampering has long been a problem, but it has only recently emerged as a prominent issue with the coverage of several dramatic cases, including the Tylenol and Gerber Baby Foods incidents.

A slightly more powerful effect has been labeled issue salience: "Heavy media emphasis on an issue or topic can move it into the top ranks of the personal agendas of the audience" (McCombs, 1977). Here, the key concept has to do with the amount of importance the person places on an issue, but not the exact ranking. Sobel's (1982) research on health communication demonstrates support for this kind of effect.

Using evidence from a public education campaign, she shows that exposure to media messages about heart health led persons to place greater importance on this issue (the intrapersonal agenda), as well as discuss the issue more frequently (the interpersonal agenda).Others (Atwood, Sohn, & Sohn, 1978; Sohn, 1978) found similar evidence that the local newspaper is effective in setting the local talking agenda.

Academic researchers Edna F. Einseidel, Kandice L. Salamone, and Fredrick P. Schneider (1984) also found agenda-setting effects as a result of exposure to crime news. Their phone survey shows that exposure to crime news is a better predictor of issue salience than is personal exposure to crime. Media attention can also influence the priorities that persons place on different existing issues. This has been the focus of the largest amount of research in the area of agenda setting. It also represents the most powerful agenda-setting effect. As McCombs says (1977), "We judge as important what the media judge as important."

Agenda-setting effects are not just limited to issues themselves. Media prominence can also influence the awareness, salience, or priority of the attributes of an issue. Sobel (1982), for example, found that media coverage of heart health led to the increased salience of certain cardiovascular risk factors. These include smoking, lack of exercise, and high blood pressure.

Einseidel et al. (1984) found agenda-setting effects as a result of exposure to crime news. Their phone survey shows that exposure to crime news is a better predictor of issue salience than is personal exposure to crime.

A PR Viewpoint. People use the media as a form of social radar. They "survey" the world through the press, television, and other mass media. Political scientist Harold D. Lasswell (1972) calls this the "surveillance" function of the media. The process of media agenda setting highlights this surveillance function. It illustrates the manner in which the media can bring an issue or event to our attention. From a PR point of view, however, one must take care to remember that the power of the media is quite limited in this sense. The issue must be newsworthy, and it must stay on the media agenda for several months for it to influence the public agendas.

Perhaps more important, one must consider the early work of scholar and journalist Robert Park (1923), who studied news as a form of knowledge. He argued that there are two forms of knowledge: knowledge about and acquaintance with. *Knowledge about* refers to a depth of information holding, while *acquaintance with* refers to a more superficial familiarity with a topic. Journalism, according to Park (and others more recently, such as Roscho, 1975), is associated more with the latter category. So, too, is the process of agenda setting associated more with Park's "acquaintance with" concept of knowledge. Thus, one cannot expect a media-based campaign to produce significant changes in knowledge about an issue. Rather, one can realistically expect only changes in the awareness or salience of issues, or the priorities people place on those issues.

Finally, issues, like consumer products, have a life cycle. There is an early stage of growth, there is a stage of maturity, and there is a stage of decline or death. Agenda setting tends to focus on the early growth stage of an issue. It deals with the initial stages of movement onto the agenda (McCombs, 1977; Watt & Vanden Bergh, 1981).

From a PR campaign planning point of view, one must consider where an issue is in its life cycle. Is it an emerging issue, or an established one? Agenda-setting issues may not apply to issues in this latter category.

Who Sets the Media Agenda?

American journalism rests on the principle of freedom of the press. This means the press will be free to publish what it deems important and free from governmental censorship. It also implies that it is the gatekeepers of the press themselves who are making the decisions about what is news and what will be reported. We assume that the members of the press determine the news agenda. How valid is this assumption?

A growing amount of research suggests that the press agendas may often simply reflect the agendas of other social actors and institutions, especially those with active PR functions. Consider the phenomenon media critic Daniel Boorstin more than 20 years ago labeled the "pseudo-event." In *The Image: A Guide to Pseudo-Events in America,* Boorstin wrote (1964), "The power to make a reportable event is thus the power to make experience." Everyday, organizations "create" events that are covered by the media as "news." These events are not spontaneous, they are carefully planned and orchestrated. In fact, they are often staged at just the right time of day to facilitate media news coverage. Organizations create these pseudo-events in order to manipulate the media. Through media coverage, they are able to distribute their message to an unsuspecting public. Examine a copy of your local newspaper. How many stories and pictures do you suppose originated as "enterprise" stories—that is, stories based solely upon the investigative efforts of a journalist? You'll probably see that many of them originated through a pseudo-event—a press conference, a labor strike, a citizen in space, or even a terroristic hijacking of a commercial airliner. Even the recent U.S. bombing of Libya was timed for television coverage during the evening network newscasts. A number of studies have shown a link between news media content and PR communication activities, including pseudo-events, press releases, and others. Professor David B. Sachsman (1976) reveals that more than one-half of all environmental stories in the San Francisco area are based on press releases, most frequently those of governmental agencies. Turk (1985) refers to this process as providing journalists with "information subsidies."

Influencing the media agenda does not always mean influencing the amount of coverage devoted to an issue. In a study (1978) of California Supreme Court decisions, Professor F. Dennis Hale examined the impact of press releases on newspaper coverage via content analysis. His study shows that press releases influenced the kinds of court decisions that were reported, but not the quantity of coverage by newspapers.

Of course, PR efforts cannot always influence media agenda. A recent content analysis (Stocking, 1985) shows that under certain circumstances, PR activities have no effect on media visibility of the organization, independent of the news value of the organization. For example, this study shows that school prestige and productivity were related to visibility of medical school research, but PR efforts were not. Turk (1985) similarly found that published information does not necessarily reflect the policy or issue priorities of the agencies involved.

Some studies have examined the factors that enhance the agenda-building process. One investigation (Williams et al., 1983) in the political arena suggests that "framing" the issue agenda provides a context that facilitates the movement of an issue onto the public agenda or higher on the agenda.

Another study (Newsom, 1983) shows that pressure groups often generate more coverage than the organizations they attack.

Professor David Weaver and graduate student Swanzy N. Elliot (1985) examined this issue on the local level. They looked at daily agendas of both the city council and the daily newspaper and found a clear link between the two. Their content analysis suggests that a prominent local news source exerts a significant influence on the local press agenda.

The Knowledge-Gap Hypothesis

Developed by Professors George A. Donohue, Clarice N. Olien, and Phillip J. Tichenor (1973), the knowledge-gap hypothesis deals with the distribution of knowledge in society. Much as there tends to be an uneven distribution of wealth in our society, Donohue et al. argue that in some circumstances knowledge tends to be unevenly distributed in our society. Since the possession and control of knowledge are critical to many organizations, this phenomenon is quite important in our understanding of public relations.

According to the research of Donohue et al., persons with high socioeconomic status (SES) tend to have more knowledge about public affairs issues than persons with low SES. Persons with low SES tend to have an "acquaintance with" these issues (see Park, 1923), but lack the depth of knowledge of the high-SES persons. This disparity is known as a "knowledge gap." This gap may occur for a variety of reasons. For instance, persons with high SES tend to be more involved in the political process (e.g., they are more likely to vote).

Donohue et al. have also shown that over time, the knowledge gap tends to widen, not narrow. The mass media disseminate information about public affairs issues, but this information is acquired unevenly. This is called the "knowledge-gap" hypothesis. This happens for several reasons. First, persons with high and low SES tend to use different media. Those with high SES are more likely to attend to print media, including newspapers and magazines. Low-SES persons are more electronically oriented. Since the print media are "information" media, while the electronic media are "entertainment" media, knowledge is acquired unevenly.

In a related fashion, persons with high and low SES tend to use the media differently. Those with high SES are often actively seeking information when attending to the media. Those with low SES are more likely to be passively processing the information, seeking diversion, escape, or entertainment.

Persons with high SES are also more likely to fall into the category of "media rich" (Chaffee & Wilson, 1977). A media rich person is one with a variety of media available in his or her home. For example, a high-SES person is likely to have more than one television (as well as a videocassette recorder), more than one radio, at least one daily newspaper subscription, and several magazine subscriptions. Meanwhile, a low-SES person is more likely to be "media poor," by comparison. He or she will probably have a television and radio, but is much less likely to have the newspaper and magazine subscriptions of his or her high-SES counterpart. Chaffee and Donna Wilson (1977) have demonstrated differences between communities that are media rich or poor. In their survey investigation, they present national and Wisconsin data that indicate diversity of agenda is higher in communities that have more than one newspaper (i.e., media rich).

Thus, the availability of media alternatives may contribute to the uneven acquisition of information. Other group characteristics may be related to the uneven acquisition of knowledge. For example, a survey reported by Cecile Gaziano (1984) of Minnesota Opinion Research shows that high levels of organized group activity are related to higher public affairs knowledge levels.

Of course, the knowledge-gap phenomenon may not always hold. Donohue et al. suggest one very important factor that may counteract the gap-widening process often observed. When the issue involves a high level of conflict, the knowledge gap may not widen; in fact, it may even narrow. The high level of conflict tends to raise the interest level of involved persons. Thus, persons of both high and low SES tend to acquire significant amounts of information about the issue. Because of the significance of Donohue et al.'s findings, numerous researchers have attempted to test the knowledge-gap hypothesis under a variety of other conditions. The Gaziano (1984) study, for example, shows that when there is a high level of organized group activity, the knowledge gap may continue to widen even when conflict exists.

Research by Professors F. Gerald Kline and James S. Ettema (1977) has confirmed Donohue et al.'s findings, but also shows another condition under which the gap may not widen. Kline and Ettema show that there may be a limit both to the amount of information available in the media and to the amount to be absorbed by the audience members. This effect is known as the "ceiling effect." When the ceiling is reached, the gap will no longer widen; it may narrow or disappear.

Finally, research by Ettema, James W. Brown, and Russell V. Leupker (1983) indicates that the knowledge gap may be limited to only certain kinds of knowledge. Their tests in a public health education campaign suggest that SES level is not related to the acquisition of heart health knowledge from the mass media. Nevertheless, since much corporate public relations involves public affairs issues, the possibility of a knowledge-gap phenomenon is well worth considering. Grunig, for example, has found knowledge-gap effects in his research on business communication. One study (Grunig, 1982) showed that only those who already knew about business and economics sought or processed information about traditional economic education programs dealing with profits and free enterprise. Meanwhile, for situations in which business has direct consequences on the population, he found most people will seek—or at least process—the information (Grunig, 1979a). His solution: establishing a two-way dialogue between business and the public (Grunig, 1982).

A Cognitive Complexity Gap?

Grunig and Ipes (1983) present evidence of a gap in cognitive complexity similar to the knowledge gap identified by Donohue et al. Their study involved an examination of active and inactive publics before and after a campaign against drunk driving. The researchers show that publics active before the campaign are likely to develop organized cognitions as a result of exposure to the campaign. Such an increase in organization seems to facilitate action. Publics inactive prior to the campaign do gain information from the campaign, but their cognitions do not increase in complexity (i.e., level of organization).

Cognitive complexity is based on the concept of schemata from psychology. Schemata are hierarchically arranged beliefs a person uses to select, interpret, and remember information (Schneider, 1985c). They are continually revised as a result of exposure to new messages—such as those in an educational campaign. For example, in the area of heart health knowledge, a person might have a relatively simple cognitive scheme before a campaign—he or she believes the main cause of heart attacks is high blood pressure, which is caused by heredity (see Figure 4.1). After the campaign, we might see a significant increase in the complexity of the schemata (see Figure 4.2). Now the person believes the main causes of heart attacks are high blood pressure, cigarette smoking, and overweight, each of which is caused not only by heredity but also by environmental factors such as a diet high in salt or a lack of exercise.

Professors Pavlik and Daniel B. Wackman (1985) examined this conceptualization of cognitive complexity in an ongoing health education campaign. Using experimental data from the Minnesota Heart Health Program, they found a significant increase in complexity of heart health knowledge as a result of campaign exposure—especially for those highly involved in heart health. Such a difference may produce a gap in cognitive complexity.

The findings of Grunig and Ipes (1983) and Pavlik and Wackman (1985) have implications for PR campaign planning. They indicate that practitioners should begin by assessing audience complexity and involvement levels prior to a campaign. Objectives and messages can be tailored for and targeted at each public, depending upon their original level of complexity and involvement. As Professor Larissa A. Schneider (1985c) points out, by understanding how new data fit existing patterns, PR people can structure messages more effectively. They can improve their newsletters, speeches, and information campaigns in general.

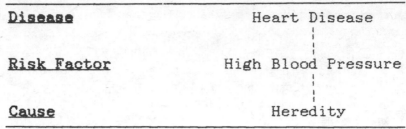

Figure 4.1 Simple Cognitive Scheme

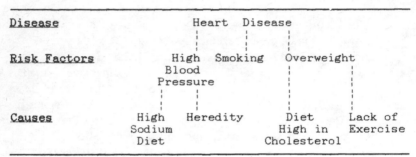

Figure 4.2 Complex Cognitive Scheme

Associationist Attitude Theory

Borrowing from the field of advertising, a number of PR researchers have begun to study "associationist attitude theory" and its usefulness in public relations. This theory is based most fundamentally upon psychological principles of beliefs. Beliefs are the characteristics or attributes of an issue or object that a person holds to be true. They are not necessarily true. For example, when Columbus set sail in the late 1400s, many people believed the world was flat. Columbus believed otherwise.

Advertising researchers have shown that consumers often develop product attitudes based upon the beliefs they link to that product. These linkage beliefs—or associations—are usually based upon images created through advertising messages.

Recent investigations of associationist attitude theory in public relations have suggested that this approach may prove quite valuable in campaign planning (Culbertson & Stempel, 1985). One study (Denbow & Culbertson, 1985) concludes that "an organization's image could be altered by associating it with desirable objects and dissociating it from negative ones." This view was anticipated by Bernays in the 1930s when he worked on behalf of the major brewers to dissociate beer from the unsavory taverns and saloons of that era (Bernays, 1986). To date, PR research in this area has relied on survey methods. Experimental research is needed to provide a rigorous testing of the applicability of associationist attitude theory to public relations. As Professors Culbertson and Guido H. Stempel suggest (1985) research is needed to study the effectiveness of belief linkage formation in predicting attitude from behavior change and formation.

The associatist approach may even be useful in identifying media for PR communications. Jeffers (1983) found that respondents in a phone survey tend to associate different values with different media. For instance, they associate a comfortable life and family security with television, while associating freedom and national security with newspapers. A study by Van Leuven (1980) indicates that value-associations may help distinguish target audiences, too. This overall approach, based upon Rokeach's (1979) notions of terminal and instrumental values, warrants further experimental research.

A Bernays Perspective

Edward Bernays was the first person to teach a course on public relations, and he was the first to emphasize the importance of the social sciences in public relations. He argues persuasively that one cannot effectively influence public opinion without first having a basic knowledge of human behavior.

He has also been one of the strongest proponents of the use of research in public relations, especially in campaign planning. Bernays suggests that research can tell us what the current situation is, and how to get from there to our ultimate goal. He elaborates (1986), "We use research to identify and correct the 'maladjustments' of public opinion, perceptions and actions to help meet organizational objectives." His career is rich in examples of research used in this fashion.

At the end of Prohibition, Bernays recently recalled (1986), he was asked by the large breweries if he could help establish beer as "the beverage of moderation." "Of course," Bernays added, "this didn't make the liquor producers very happy." The brewers wanted to disassociate beer from taverns and bars, which were not seen in a very favorable light at the time. Many taverns were dirty, infested with mice, and people associated them with gangsters.

"I hired a graduate student to conduct some extensive research on beer," Bernays said. "We learned that beer had been very popular among many American Revolutionary War heroes, including George Washington. One of Washington's favorite dishes was a beer cake

Martha used to bake for him." From this research, Bernays compiled a recipe book filled with beer dishes popular among early American heroes. This recipe book was mailed to all the legislatures in the United States, urging them to recognize beer as the beverage of moderation—and to allow the sale of beer in grocery stores.

Was this campaign successful? Today, more than half the states in the union allow the sale of beer in grocery stores. Without research, this might not be the case.

Another time, Bernays was working for the Pullman Co. His research revealed that passengers were calling all the porters "an indiscriminate 'George,' which affected the morale of the porters." Bernays's solution? He recommended installing name placards in each car indicating the correct identity of each porter. Passengers immediately began calling the porters by their actual names, and the morale problem disappeared.

These examples are more than anomalies.

The Third-Person Effect of Communication

Most PR programs are designed to influence the receiver of the message directly. For example, programs are often designed to generate public support for a company by instituting a corporate advertising campaign. The strategy is that those who see the message will be favorably influenced by its content or the source. In a recent article, W. Phillips Davison (1982) has outlined a somewhat different perspective on the persuasion process. He calls it the third-person effect of communication. Consider the following vignette:

> In 1949 or 1950, a young historian at Princeton University discovered some unusual Marine Corps documents from World War II. Stepping across the hall, he described his find to an even younger sociologist, Davison:
>
> "You're supposed to know something about public opinion. What do you make of this? There was a service unit consisting of Negro troops with white officers on Iwo Jima Island in the Pacific. The Japanese learned about the location of this unit and sent planes over with propaganda leaflets. These leaflets stressed the theme that this was a white man's war and that the Japanese had no quarrel with colored peoples. They said, more or less, 'Don't risk your life for the white man. Give yourself up at the next opportunity, or just desert. Don't take chances.' The next day that unit was withdrawn."
>
> "Why do you find this so interesting?" asked the sociologist.

"Because I can't find any evidence that the propaganda had an effect on the troops at all. But it sure had an effect on the white officers. The leaflets seem to have caused a substantial reshuffle of personnel."

The young sociologist came up with an answer, but it was an unsatisfactory one. He suggested that the white officers may have acted on their guilt feelings, or that the armed forces tend to prefer solutions that involve action.

Years later, after observing the communication process in a variety of mass media settings, Davison formulated the following hypothesis to explain the events on Iwo Jima: "People will tend to overestimate the influence that mass communications have on the attitudes and behavior of others." Thus, a communication may lead to action, not because of its effect on the ostensible audience, but because others (third persons) believe it will influence its audience. In the case of the Black troops on Iwo Jima, the white officers may have thought the propaganda would influence the troops. Consequently, they may have withdrawn the troops in order to avoid any possible desertions or surrenders.

In his 1982 article, Davison further documents the third-person effect in a series of four small laboratory experiments. Although on a small scale, each experiment confirms the hypothesis. For example, one study involved a "good-natured group" of 33 graduate students at Columbia University in 1978 shortly after the New York state election of that year. Davison administered a two-part questionnaire—part one dealing with the feelings of New Yorkers in general, and part two dealing with the subjects' personal feelings. One of the items in the first section read as follows:

As you probably know, Governor Carey repeatedly called on Mr. Duryea [the Republican challenger] to make his income tax returns public, and used Mr. Duryea's failure to do so as a major campaign theme. About how much influence do you think this had on the way New Yorkers voted in the gubernatorial election? Please indicate this by making a mark at the appropriate point on the scale below.

The scale ran from 0 (no influence at all) to 7 (very great influence). An item at the end of the second section read:

And how about Governor Carey's emphasis on Mr. Duryea's failure to make his income tax returns public? If you had been a New York voter (or if you actually were a New York voter), how much influence do you think this would have had (or actually did have) on your vote in the gubernatorial election? Please indicate this by making a mark at the appropriate point on the scale below [the same scale as in the first question was used].

The results were clear. Respondents tended to estimate a much greater effect on New Yorkers in general (48%) than on themselves (6%).

Implications for Public Relations. There are many phenomena in our daily lives that may involve the third-person effect of communication and that have strong implications for public relations. Consider the following scenario: A news story reports that there will soon be a shortage of some particular consumer good. Chances are there will soon be a shortage if for no other reason than many consumers will rush out and buy large quantities. If you ask them why, the answer is likely to be that they are concerned about the effects of these reports on other people. They want to stock up before the hoarders remove all goods from the shelves.

Such news stories may affect the behavior not only of consumers but of organizations as well. For instance, an item in the *New York Times* (September 16, 1975) reported that manufacturers of products sold in aerosol cans quickly changed to spray and squeeze containers when news stories about the possibly dangerous effects of aerosol on the earth's atmosphere began to appear. While there are many possible explanations for this corporate reaction, one possibility is that manufacturers expected the negative publicity to turn consumers against aerosol cans and were hoping to minimize any losses.

This view has many implications for PR planning. For example, PR programs are often aimed at legislative decision makers. Strategies usually entail lobbying or sending messages directly to the legislators. While such strategies are often effective and essential, an equally important mechanism might involve the third-person effect of communication. Specifically, legislators might be strongly influenced by the public response they anticipate as a result of certain news items.

As Davison points out, many scholars also have speculated that "experts" are especially likely to overestimate the effects of mass communications. Tichenor, Donohue, and Olien (1977), for example, interviewed an expert on a locally controversial issue. His view, they said, "is typical, in the sense that it includes the belief that media affect people in general [except] the individual who has specialized expertise."

Davison argues that we are all experts on those subjects that matter to us, because we have information not available to other people. "This information may not be factual or technical in nature; it may have to do with our own experiences. Other people, we reason, do not know what we know. Therefore, they are more likely to be influenced by the media."

To what extent is this process true of PR professionals? If PR persons view themselves as experts in the art or science of human persuasion, they may very well overestimate the effect of their communications on the audience. This may lead to unrealistic program goals or misperceptions of the effects of PR efforts. In any case, this highlights the need to conduct systematic research before, during, and after a campaign in order to specify the potential and actual effects of a communications program.

QUESTIONING TRADITIONAL APPROACHES

A growing amount of research has begun to question the traditional assumptions of public relations. As reported by Tichenor et al. (1977), "Recent research and community literature generally do not support some of the most cherished notions about public information and public relations." Research on community organizations, for example, suggests that structural factors may override any communication activities.

Community Research

Tichenor et al.'s own research (1977) on community relations, for example, indicates that the goal of compatibility between organization and community "is quite unrealistic in many situations." The researchers argue that three factors may determine how "realistic" the compatibility goal is in community relations. They are (1) community conflict processes, including any that have involved the organization in the past; (2) communications structure, especially the nature and use of the local newspaper and broadcast media; and (3) community structure, including the level of pluralism in its power structures, the type of leadership structure, and the value system regarding dependence on outside agencies or corporations.

To illustrate these concepts, consider a type of conflict that has emerged in recent years (Tichenor et al., 1977). It usually involves a struggle for community control, between the community and an agency or corporation that is controlled elsewhere. Tichenor et al. state, "Often the primary issue is control rather than merit or demerit of the proposal." It is often "a contest over information and its interpretation."

A prominent issue in Minnesota provides a good example. For more than a decade there has been political pressure to prohibit all commercial logging and motorboating in the Boundary Waters Canoe Area (BWCA), a wilderness area on the border between Minnesota and Canada. Most of this pressure has arisen from urban areas of Minnesota and the rest of the nation. Residents of BWCA communities often see environmentalist arguments as rationalizations for "preserving unspoiled playgrounds for wealthy urbanites." The wealthy urbanites, localites complain, are unconcerned about the economic and social survival of the communities in the BWCA. The battle is an urban-rural one, and "environmental concerns are secondary as far as local communities are concerned."

The traditional PR tool in a case such as the one described above has been increased communication. Unfortunately, research (Cain, Katz, & Rosenthal, 1969) has shown that a high level of public communication does not always lead to increased support for a newly introduced program. Donohue, Olien, and Tichenor (1974) add that increased understanding does not guarantee support for a program; "some of the most vocal objectors to a given program are the best informed about it and about the advocate's point of view." Other research (Wilson, 1973) also shows that neither early support from community leaders nor public participation in decision making will ensure the acceptance of an idea or program.

The research of Tichenor and his colleagues also shows that the role of the media in the conflict process varies with the size and nature of the community (Donohue, Olien, & Tichenor, 1985b). Larger communities tend to be more pluralistic, diverse, or heterogeneous. While small, rural communities tend to be more homogeneous. In the larger, more pluralistic community, the media are more likely to report any conflict that arises than are the media in a small community. In a small community, the local media or press are more akin to a "corporate newsletter," promoting community goodwill because the press is closely tied to the existing power structure in that community.

These community differences tend to be recognized by community leaders and media gatekeepers. In a recent (1985a) face-to-face survey, Donohue, Olien, and Tichenor found that leaders in more pluralistic regions are more likely to perceive newspapers as taking the initiative in reporting conflict. This is an accurate perception. The study also indicated that important as newspapers and other mass media are in social conflict, they are secondary to other forms of social organization as far as conflict is concerned. This is not necessarily the case as far as public perceptions are concerned. One study (Smith, 1984), for instance, found that members of the general public in Louisville, Kentucky, considered television and newspapers the most influential of 12 community groups.

Community pluralism is also related to media use and perceptions (Tichenor, Nnaemeka, Olien, and Donohue, 1977; Olien, Donohue, and Tichenor, 1978). Those in large, nonpluralistic communities tend to see media content (especially television) as more realistic than their rural counterparts. Those in the rural community are more likely to read a weekly newspaper and more likely to prefer TV as a source of news.

Professors Charles T. Salmon and Jung-Sook Lee (1983) used a community structural approach to study perceptions of newspaper fairness. They conducted a telephone survey of 196 persons in a small, homogeneous community and a large, pluralistic community. The results indicate that residents of a community perceive their local newspaper as more fair than newspapers in general—but structural factors affect individual attitudes. *Localites*—those who have an orientation toward their own community and read only their local newspaper—see their local newspaper as significantly more fair than newspapers in general. In contrast, *cosmopolites*—persons oriented to organizations and events beyond their hometown and who read more than a local newspaper—are less likely to see their hometown newspaper as more fair. Salmon and Lee suggest that cosmopolites tend to have diverse interests, and a local newspaper does not meet their needs well. Thus, the local newspaper is seen as less fair. Cosmopolites are more likely to be found in a large, pluralistic community, but may reside in small, more homogeneous towns as well.

Such evidence has clear implications for PR campaign planning. Depending on the nature of the public—localite or cosmopolite—a local newspaper may be more or less effective in delivering an organization's message. Recent research from other areas also indicates a need to reassess some of the basic premises of the field. One such area involves internal relations.

Internal Relations

One of the most important issues in internal relations is how to communicate with employees effectively. Pavlik et al. (1982) attempted to address one aspect of this issue by applying a theoretical approach known as "uses and gratifications" research to the practical problem of employee newsletter readership.

The Uses and Gratifications Approach. The uses and gratifications approach is an attempt to look at the process of communication from the point of view of the receiver—in this case the employee. It asks: Why do employees read company newsletters? What purpose does the employee have for reading a company newsletter? This view is a departure from the traditional view of employee communications, in which newsletters are thought of as serving the purposes of management. These purposes have included building goodwill between management and the rank and file, keeping employees informed of changes in company policies and practices, and developing a homogeneous social network among employees.

Fundamentally, the uses and gratifications approach is based on the assumption that the audience is active in its use of the media. Rather than viewing audience members as completely passive recipients of media messages, the approach suggests that people are often purposive in their use of the media (Jeffres, 1975).

This perspective is based in part on Lazarsfeld et al.'s (1944) concept of "selective exposure" and Raymond A. Bauer's (1964) notion of the "obstinate audience." Professors Lazarsfeld and Bauer empirically demonstrated more than 20 years ago that people have various social and psychological predispositions that lead them to use the media in different ways.

Pavlik et al. (1982) applied these ideas to the study of employee newsletter readership at Honeywell, Inc., a large organization specializing in control devices. Honeywell manufactures everything from thermostats for heating systems to guidance systems for military weapons. It employs more than 30,000 workers worldwide, with its corporate headquarters in Minneapolis, Minnesota. Honeywell regularly publishes two employee newsletters: *The Ciculator,* a localized weekly for employees in the Minneapolis area, and *The World,* an international, biweekly for all of its employees. Both newsletters are distributed free of charge to employees.

The study by Pavlik et al. (1982) is based on two parts: a content analysis of newsletters from five different organizations in the Twin Cities area, including Honeywell, and a mail survey of 95 Honeywell employees. These employees are largely from managerial, professional, and supervisory positions at Honeywell's executive offices in the Twin Cities.

Three Content Types. The content analysis reveals three major content themes in the newsletters: employee social relations content (e.g., personnel announcements, employee vital statistics, features on individual employees, social event announcements, and articles on social activities); company news (e.g., financial news, employee investment program news, stories on products and services, and general company news); and job-related content (e.g., work-related news and stories about employee benefits). These findings are consistent with those of Grunig (1977).

Readership Patterns. Based on the three newsletter content areas, Pavlik et al. developed three readership scales. Readership of job-related content is the highest of the three scales, with almost two-thirds of the respondents reporting high readership. That is, about two-thirds read all the job-related content in any single issue of the newsletter. About one-third of the respondents report high readership of employee social relations content. Lowest readership is reported for company news, with only one-fourth of the respondents falling into the high readership category of this scale.

These results somewhat contradict traditional notions of employee newsletters. For many organizations, the employee newsletter has been designed to accomplish the goals of building goodwill, enhancing the social climate of the organization, and informing employees. Thus, newsletter content has tended to emphasize company news and employee social relations content, with little emphasis on job-related content. Pavlik et al.'s research indicates that such an emphasis may be neglecting the interests or needs of the employee, and leading to lower levels of newsletter readership.

Applying the uses and gratifications theoretical model in this study supports this interpretation. The data show that factors such as length of employment, position in the decision-making hierarchy, or level of career aspirations are not directly related to newsletter readership. However, when an employee's purposes (i.e., uses) for reading the newsletter are considered, certain patterns begin to emerge. For example, an employee with high career aspirations tends to read the newsletter to keep track of changes in management and to improve his or her advancement possibilities. This leads him or her to have higher readership of company news. These results suggest that the most effective newsletter would be one designed to meet not only the needs of management but the "uses" employees as well.

Uses and Gratifications and PR Programs. A number of other studies have attempted to link the uses and gratifications approach to PR programs (Netteberg, 1984; Snyder, 1978). One investigation provides a partial replication of the Pavlik et al. (1982) study. Here, Professor Kermit Netteberg (1984) combined content analysis and readership research to evaluate a church publication. His study confirms the usefulness of the uses and gratifications theoretical approach as a way of diagnosing the effectiveness of a communication vehicle. With the uses and gratifications approach Netteberg measured three dimensions of newsletter readership—regularity, time spent, and articles recalled. The results indicate that the newsletter is meeting its ultimate goal: to communicate with the people who are the major force of the church.

Understanding newsletters, especially church newsletters, may be enhanced by taking a "community" perspective. If we look at an organization—say a church—as a community, we may better understand why and how members read a newsletter. Professors Robert J. Weis and Keith R. Stamm (1984) found that church members often vary in the degree to which they "identify" with the community. Especially important is the transitional stage of "settling into" an organization. It is at this stage that an audience can be most effectively segmented, and a newsletter can be effectively used to facilitate this process.

A Qualitative View. Professor Leonard J. Snyder (1978) looks at the uses and gratifications approach and public relations from a somewhat different perspective. Rather than using the traditional quantitative social science approach, his study employs an approach known as "phenomenological sociology." This approach is a more qualitative, humanistic approach to research.

As applied to uses and gratifications, it suggests that the motivation for media use should be identified not by the observer (i.e., the researcher), but by the audience members. Thus, PR people using this approach should use "open-ended" questioning with as little predetermined structure as possible to allow the audience members to answer freely. This kind of research should be conducted prior to initiating a campaign.

Finally, the approach would be most useful when a majority of the population has identifiable motivations, especially when they are known to be receptive to messages of high information utility.

Criticisms of the Approach. A number of scholars have criticized the uses and gratifications approach (e.g., Garramone, 1985). They argue it is atheoretical—purely descriptive—and provides little real explanatory power. Professor Gina M. Garramone (1985) contends that few studies have explored the relationship between audience motivations and the criteria audience members use for selecting messages to which they attend.

Consequently, a number of researchers have attempted to respond to these criticisms in their research. In response to her own criticism, Garramone (1985) examined telephone survey data on the 1984 presidential campaign. She found that people selectively attend to presidential campaign information based on editorial format. Practitioner Harold DeBock (1980) and Garramone (1984a, 1984b) also provide evidence of the validity of the approach through cross-national validation and replication across media. Through survey research, Daniel J. McDonald and Carroll J. Glynn (1984) demonstrate the stability of gratification measures of surveillance and communication utility.

International scholars Mark R. Levey and Sven Windahl (1984) studied audience activity and media gratifications in a personal survey of 390 persons in Vaxjo, Sweden. Interviewing parents to assess their children's media habits, the research team obtained a 78% response rate. The study reveals two critical dimensions in media activity—(1) selectivity and (2) the phase of communication. *Selectivity* refers to the audience orientation to the media (i.e., level of involvement). *Communication phase* refers to a temporal sequence—preexposure, exposure, or postexposure. By combining these dimensions, the researchers suggest, we can identify different audience types, or publics.

A Structural View of Internal Relations. Internal relations programs have often been based on the assumption that communication can increase worker satisfaction, morale, or even productivity. Professors J. David Pincus and Robert Rayfield (1986), for example, present evidence to support this idea. Using data from a survey of 327 nurses at an East Coast hospital, they found that employees' perceptions of top management communication are positively related to their job satisfac.

In contrast, a study by Grunig (1986) suggests that the communication-job satisfaction relationship may be a spurious one. Based upon more than 1000 personal interviews with employees of the Maryland State Department of Education, his study shows that organizational structure may be a much more important factor than employee communication in determining job satisfaction. In fact, Grunig's data indicate that communication may have virtually no effect on job satisfaction, once organizational structure is controlled for. Structural factors include sociologist Jerald Hage's (1980) concepts of organizational complexity, stratification, centralization, and formalization.

Reconsidering PR Goals: The Coorientational Model

The purpose of public relations has long been to influence public opinion. From Ivy Lee to Lee Iacocca, PR activities have been designed to persuade. Professors Allen Center and Frank E. Walsh (1981) offer this definition, "Public relations is the planned effort to influence opinion through good character and responsible performance, based upon mutually satisfactory two-way communication."

This view of public relations, however, is a narrow one. Many communication activities of an organization need not be designed to persuade, but rather, to shape perceptions. David Finn, Chief Executive Officer for Ruder, Finn and Rotman, argues (1984) that one important PR function is to square public perceptions with reality. This does not necessarily imply influencing attitudes.

Practitioner Joyce F. Jones (1975) suggests the four following steps when conducting a PR audit:

(1) finding out what "we" think
(2) finding out what "they" think
(3) evaluating the disparity between the two points of views
(4) recommending a comprehensive communications program aimed at closing the gap

Broom (1977) makes a similar argument. He states, "Viewing two-way communication as the key process through which corporate-public relations are adjusted and maintained, it is in developing similar definitions of issues and accurate perceptions of each others' views—developing a consensus of understanding—that public relations makes its most important contribution." In this manner, he contends that the interpersonal coorientation measurement model developed by Professors Jack M. McLeod and Steven H. Chaffee (1973) can be fruitfully applied to improve our understanding of public relations.

Interpersonal coorientation measurement is concerned with how two individuals view a situation, as well as each one's perceptions of the other's views. In Figure 4.3, the boxes on the left refer to person A's view of some object or issue, for example nuclear power, as well as A's estimate of person B's view of that issue. The arrow connecting these boxes represents "congruency," a measure of the similarity between A's view of nuclear power and the view he or she attributes to B. The right side of the figure refers to the same measures, only for person B.

The remaining arrows in this figure represent the interpersonal relationships between persons A and B. The arrow labeled agreement represents the extent to which A and B have the same attitudes toward the issue, nuclear power. Shared understanding refers to the extent to which they define the issue in the same manner. Accuracy represents the extent to which each person correctly perceives the other's views toward the issue.

As Broom demonstrates, one can easily substitute "corporation" for person A, and "public" for person B, thus adapting this measurement model to public relations (see Figure 4.4). Continuing with the same

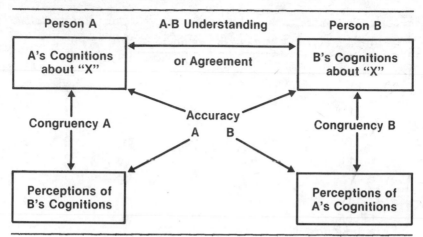

Figure 4.3 Coorientation Measurement Model (after Chaffee & McLeod, 1973)

issue of nuclear power, let's assume our corporation is a public utilities corporation and our public is an activist environmental group. The boxes on the right would represent the utility's views of nuclear power, as well as the views it attributes to the environmental group. The arrow connecting these boxes would represent the similarity between the utility's views and the views it attributes to the environmental group. The right side of the figure would represent parallel measures for the environmental group.

The remaining arrows in this figure represent the relationships between the utility and the environmental group. The arrow labeled agreement represents the extent to which the utility and the environmental group have the same evaluations of the issue, nuclear power. Shared understanding refers to the extent to which they define the issue in the same manner. Accuracy represents the extent to which each organization correctly perceives the other's views toward the issue.

AN EVOLVING VIEW OF PUBLIC RELATIONS

Since the early days of Bernays and Lee, public relations has been defined as a form of persuasive communication. This is clearly reflected in the title and pages of Bernays's classic PR text, *The Engineering of Consent* (1955).

Too much recent research now suggests, however, that the traditional goals of public relations may be unobtainable in many situations or may

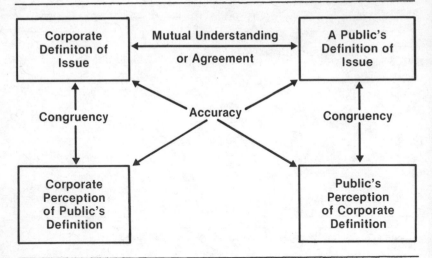

Figure 4.4 Corporate-Public Consensus of Understanding Model (after Broom, 1977)

require tools beyond those of communication alone. Jan Jaffe (1983) reports that advertising has become the business of "image management." (Jaffe is the Director of Research at Backer & Spielvogel, Inc., a New York-based advertising agency best known for its humorous Miller Lite Beer campaign featuring former professional athletes.) Public relations seems to be following the same evolutionary track. One might say public relations has evolved into the business of "relationship management."

Jaffe adds that all products have an image. The role of advertising, she explains, is to manage that image, to shape it in the planned direction. The task facing public relations may be the same. Every organization has a relationship with its public (or publics). The role of public relations is to manage that relationship or nurture it in the desired direction.

The role of research in PR program planning has begun to change, too. AT&T's PR Research Director Gary Schmermund explains (1986):

Historically, research was used to take the temperature. Someone else diagnosed the patient. Research has been moving closer to the decision-making process. It has moved more and more into the interpretation and recommendation process. There is also a cross-over from communication recommendations into policy recommendations. There's simply no way of sorting it out.

SUMMARY

Summarizing the findings of recent research, we can see at least three issues emerging. First, it may take more than communication to manage a relationship. Communication can accomplish only so much in today's society. It no longer has the power to influence public opinion the way it could in days of P. T. Barnum or Ivy Lee. The role of communication today is more often limited to building mutual understanding (which is often of vital importance). Instead, relationship management may require corporate action or change. Public relations—especially the research function—must play a role in shaping an organization's course of action, how it is structured, and its decision-making process. Public relations must be a part of the management of that organization. As Professors Norman R. Nager and T. Harrell Allen (1984) point out, PR practitioners must implement "management by objectives (MBO)." Related to this is the rapidly growing area of issues management. It also suggests a movement beyond the traditional journalistic model. Furthermore, communication must be more than a one-way flow; it must be a two-way process, a dialogue. This is true for both internal and external relations.

Second, much of what PR efforts traditionally have been designed to achieve may be unrealistic. In many situations compatibility between the organization and the home community may be impossible. Research is vitally important in identifying which goals are realistic.

Third, there must be an integration of theory and practice. Most research on public relations is concerned with problems in the field. Negative publicity, communication campaign effectiveness, the "professional" status of the PR practitioner are just a few examples. Because of the practical focus of such investigations, the research generally has not involved the use or development of theory. Instead, most studies are descriptive. They suggest when to use photographs, how to assure the newsworthiness of a press release, or what skills are needed for a successful career in public relations. These studies serve an important purpose, but they are limited in terms of generalizability. Since they deal with specific problems, they must be repeated frequently as circumstances change or when the problem is slightly different.

Basic research is an attempt to solve this dilemma. Basic research is theoretical. It involves the development of concepts and the testing of hypotheses. This "theory" can be applied to a variety of situations, and thus has more generalizability than descriptive research.

In recent years, a growing number of investigators have attempted to conduct basic research on public relations. For example, Grunig has looked at internal relations from a structural point of view, while Broom has developed a coorientational approach to PR planning. This research is particularly valuable because it involves the application of theoretical principles to practical problems in public relations. Others have conducted basic communication with clear implications for public relations. McCombs, for example, has studied the agenda-setting function of the media. The future of public relations is dependent on the continued growth of this basic research.

5

RESEARCH UNDONE
(WHAT THEY FAILED TO STUDY)

We will now turn our attention to what scholars have failed to study about public relations.

Most of this book discusses selected findings and implications of systematic research on public relations. But what of research that has not been done, the areas of possible study neglected or omitted from the research agenda? Unfortunately, just as it is easier to describe what we have seen than what we have not, so it is much easier to identify what has been studied, than what has not.

There are at least three ways to approach this problem. First, we can look for holes in the three major thematic areas of the research on public relations. We can do this effectively by examining the existing research in relation to the field of public relations. Second, we can look for themes that are not included in the research at all. This is a more difficult task, but can be done by taking a broader view of communication research in general—and seeing how PR research fits in. Finally, we can look at the methods of research that have not been used. Sometimes the way research is conducted is at least as important as what is studied.

HOLES IN THEMATIC AREAS

The themes of PR research are applied, basic, and introspective. Applied research—including both strategic and evaluation—has been the most voluminous, with more than half the studies falling in this area. The research has dealt with various communication techniques and program areas of public relations. One issue that has received no significant systematic research attention is the role of the computer in public relations. Although Professor William R. Oates (1985) discusses the importance of this new communications medium, there have been only two studies of its effectiveness (Harris et al., 1985; Pavlik, 1986).These studies, however, mark only a beginning. Considerably more research is needed to study this new technology in its capacity as communications medium, electronic data base, teaching tool, and more.

Another important area of applied research that has received scant attention is the creative component—the message. Canadian scholar Seymour Hamilton (1986) has outlined a conceptual framework for studying the aesthetic aspect of the PR message, but systematic research is needed to test it.

Evaluation research has been receiving increased attention, with a number of studies being conducted in the past year (Bissland, 1986; Dozier, 1986). These studies have tended to focus on how evaluation research is conducted, or the kinds of effects PR campaigns have elicited. What has been missing is an answer to the broad question: What can public relations contribute to overall organizational effectiveness? This question, however, is the focus of a major five-year research grant funded by the IABC. Headed by Grunig, the investigation will involve surveys of about 300 organizations in the United States, Canada, and Great Britain, as well as detailed case studies. This study is breaking ground for an important area of research.

Scholars conducting basic research have been concerned with generating a fundamental body of knowledge upon which the field of public relations can rest. As the term suggests, public relations is concerned mainly with two things: the public and relationships. While there has been much basic research on the public (e.g., Grunig, 1976), there has been comparatively little research on relationships. Grunig's (1984) research on the level of symmetry—or balance of effects— between an organization and its publics represents the most significant work in this area. Furthermore, there has been essentially no research to date employing the "relationship" as the primary unit of analysis (Pavlik & Salmon, 1984). The unit of analysis more typically involves the individual in survey research or the article in content analysis.

The basic body of knowledge in public relations requires further research on the "relationship" component of "public relations." Perhaps more importantly, PR research will benefit from increased attention to structural factors in the organizational environment. The structure of a corporate organization, a public, or the environment itself all promise to explain much about public relations and the public opinion process.

Introspective research has touched on many areas, including PR education, ethics, and standards of the profession and practitioner roles. Unfortunately, most of this "sociological" research has been purely descriptive—telling us how many women are now working in public relations, how much they are earning or what they studied in college. The only substantial theoretical work in this area has been that dealing with practitioner roles (e.g., Broom, 1977, 1982). While there have been some recent attempts to develop a theoretical view of practitioner ethics (e.g., Ryan & Martinson, 1984), considerably more work is needed to enhance our understanding of the "sociology" of public relations. Media sociologists, for example, demonstrate that news just doesn't happen—it is manufactured (e.g., Tunstall, 1977). The role of public relations in this process and the "manufacturing" of PR communications is an important area of future research.

One important sociological area that merits at least the attention of PR educators is the phenomenon of "social control" in PR organizations. Every organization exercises social control over its members—sociologist Warren Breed (1955) first detailed this process in the newsroom, and media economist Vincent P. Norris (1983) later identified it in advertising agencies. How do PR organizations influence the attitudes and behaviors of those who work in them? This is a vital research question for the future of the profession and the individuals seeking careers in it.

Agency-client relationships and their management is another related area in need of further research. Wackman, Salmon, and Salmon (1986) have conceptualized the agency-client relationship as a conjugal one, but this research has focused on advertising and merits further study in public relations.

CRITICAL RESEARCH: AN UNEXPLORED TERRITORY

Almost all research on public relations is designed either to advance the profession or to improve our understanding of public relations in society. With only a few exceptions in the area of introspective research, critical research has been virtually nonexistent. The critical research that is conducted is more often offered as a vehicle for improving the profession, rather than questioning its role or function in society. Researchers rarely examine the negative consequences of public relations in society.

The same can be said of public relations' sister media-support institution, advertising. Most research on advertising is designed to improve our understanding of its effects in society, the way it functions. While some study the potentially harmful effects of advertising on children (Ward, Wackman, & Wartella, 1977), or the amount of information in advertising (Resnick & Stern, 1977), rarely is the institution itself questioned. Many critical researchers tend to be Marxist Europeans—few are American. One reason for the low level of critical research in these fields lies in the nature of those doing the research.

Most researchers studying advertising or public relations in the United States are either practitioners in those fields or academics with at least some professional background in or identification with those fields. Furthermore, the journals they publish in are typically devoted to "applied" research, not "critical" studies. This brings an inherent bias into the research process.

One leading American scholar who has examined advertising from a critical perspective is Vincent P. Norris—a communications professor with no professional advertising experience. His central thesis is that national consumer advertising accomplishes few or even none of the prosocial goals that it purports to accomplish.

Advertisers claim that advertising informs consumers so they can make knowledgeable decisions, lowers prices by fostering competition, and provides the necessary financial base for the media to operate. Through systematic research, Norris has attempted to show that none of these claims is true. For his investigations show that a product can be distributed and sold on a national level with no advertising—and still show a substantial profit (Norris, 1982, 1984). Similarly, his research using an economic analysis clearly shows that magazines without advertising can be sold at a lower price and at a higher level of profitability than those with advertising (Norris, 1984). He uses the profitable *Mad* magazine as a case study. At a recent dinner, I happened to be seated next to Norris and asked him whether his ideas about advertising could be applied to public relations. Norris responded, "Even more so!"

"Why?" I queried.

"Because," Norris answered, "at least in advertising, everything is out in the open. Unlike public relations, everyone knows advertising when they see or hear it. We know how much is spent on advertising each year. We know what advertising is designed to do." Public relations, by contrast, is vague and nebulous. There is no clear, agreed-upon purpose to public relations; it varies from situation to situation.

Critical research is much needed in public relations. We need to examine the institution itself. What positive functions does public relations serve in society? To what extent do PR efforts actually inform, and to what extent are they merely veiled persuasion?

RESEARCH METHODS NOT USED

Most systematic research on public relations has employed either survey or content-analytic methods. While these methods are useful for some research questions, they are not well suited for the very important issue of cause-and-effect.

Basic research, evaluation research, and even introspective research are often concerned with the effect of one variable (or set of variables) on another. What effect, for instance, can be attributed to a PR campaign? To answer such a question satisfactorily requires specially suited research methods, such as laboratory or field experimentation (what are generally called observational methods). While certain statistical analysis procedures can approximate a causal design (e.g., path analysis), they are not a perfect substitute.

The existing research also has suffered from an overuse of mail surveys, and underuse of personal interviewing. While inexpensive, mail questionnaires cannot elicit the same kind of information as the personally administered questionnaires.

SUMMARY

We have suggested a number of "holes" in the research on public relations. These holes include gaps in the four thematic areas of PR research, as well as research themes that have not been examined at all. We have also examined the holes in the research methods used to date.

While the areas covered in this discussion do not represent all the holes in PR research, they do indicate some of the largest ones.

6

AN EMERGING PARADIGM: GENERAL SYSTEM THEORY

Understanding public relations is aided by an emerging organizational view of the field—general system theory.

Thomas Kuhn (1970) talks about paradigms of science. Paradigms, explains this philosopher of science, are dominant views or theoretical perspectives in a field. In 1492, the dominant view—or paradigm—held that the world was flat. If anyone sailed too far, he or she would fall off the earth. Columbus set out to challenge this view, when he set sail for the Far East—by sailing to the west. Eventually, a new, more accurate view replaced the old paradigm.

In many ways, science still works in this fashion. Paradigms are established, scientists conduct research to challenge or confirm those views, and new theories emerge.

During the past decade, a number of scholars have conducted research to build a theoretical understanding of public relations (e.g., Broom & Dozier, 1986; Ehling, 1984; Grunig, 1984; Grunig & Grunig, 1986; Trujillo & Toth, 1986). Emerging from this systematic research is a PR paradigm based on general system theory.

GENERAL SYSTEM THEORY

General system "theory" is more a perspective or general approach than a theory per se (Bertalanffy, 1968). It is based on the view that a set of individual objects or entities are often interrelated to form a whole—or system.

Theorists distinguish between closed and open systems (Bertalanffy, 1968). A closed system has no interaction with its environment and generally applies to physical systems that have no life-sustaining qualities. Open systems do interact with their environment, exchanging inputs and outputs and adapting to changes in the environment. Open systems are applied to life-sustaining systems, such as biological or social systems. PR theorists have generally applied the "open systems" concept in their work in this area (e.g., Grunig & Grunig, 1986).

Any system consists of at least four things (Bertalanffy, 1968). First, there are *objects*. These are the various parts or members of the set, such as the departments that make up a corporate system. Second, we can identify the *attributes* of the system and its objects. Third, systems exist in an area surrounded by an *environment*. Finally, there are *relationships* between and among the objects in the system, as well as between the system and the environment. This is the focus of the largest amount of PR research.

Social scientists studying general system theory contend that biological, psychological, and social systems (i.e., open systems) have a number of common qualities, many of which form the basis for PR research. For example, systems are by definition *whole*. They are not merely a collection of unrelated parts, but rather an integrated whole. Because the parts are interrelated, every part is to a degree *interdependent*. Thus, a change in one part causes change throughout the system. A system is also *hierarchical,* typically consisting of various subsystems. One subsystem may subsume others, much as in many corporations the marketing department subsumes both advertising and public relations. Open systems are also *teleological,* or goal-oriented. They have some purpose. This purpose directs or controls the behavior of the system and its elements. The study of this process is called *cybernetics.*

Since open systems by definition interact with their environment, they also possess the quality of *interchange*. Thus, many study the inputs and outputs between an open system and its environment.

An open system must also maintain balance or *homeostasis*. This quality is similar to the function of a thermostat, which uses feedback from its environment to help maintain a relatively constant room temperature (or equilibrium). Homeostasis, or maintaining balance between an organization and its publics, is often one of the primary functions of public relations. Open systems also change and adapt. Because they exist in a changing environment, they must do so to survive. Public relations often plays a key role in the adaptive behavior of an organization. Since open systems are goal-directed, finality occurs when that goal is achieved. Open systems, however, possess an additional quality of *equifinality*. Equifinality is the idea that a goal may be achieved through a variety of ways and from various starting points.

GENERAL SYSTEM THEORY
AND PUBLIC RELATIONS

Using the general system theory perspective, a PR department can be seen as a subsystem within a complex open system. It is one element of the system, interconnected with the other subsystems. To a certain extent it is constrained or affected by their actions. Dozier (1986) maintains that the PR subsystem "engages in boundary scanning, gathering information from outside the organization's boundary to help the organization adapt to its environment." In the language of system theory, environmental scanning activities (i.e., research and other information gathering) serve as inputs, while communication activities are the PR subsystem outputs.

In many organizations, public relations is formally delegated responsibility for maintaining or regulating relationships both within and outside the organization—a major function in open system theory. A number of scholars have recognized this quality (Broom, 1986; Grunig, 1984; Grunig & Grunig, 1986; Porter, 1986). Grunig has given considerable attention to this issue. His research has led him to identify four models of PR behavior based upon this open system perspective.

Four PR Models

Originally outlined by Grunig and Hunt (1984), these models are (1) press agentry/publicity, (2) public information, (3) two-way asymmetric, and (4) two-way symmetric. These models represent the historical evolution of public relations and vary largely in terms of their purpose, style of communication, and use of research.

Press agentry/publicity represents the earliest form of public relations and is closely tied to advertising. Its sole purpose is to promote an individual, organization, or product. The flow of information is largely one way, from the press agent to the public. Research is used only on an informal basis to monitor the use of publicity in the press or to gauge attendance at pseudo-events.

One step up the evolutionary ladder is the public information model. Communication is still a one-way flow, from the organization to the public, but the purpose is the dissemination of information, not propaganda. Research, although still little used, tends to be somewhat different in nature. In the public information model, research often takes the form of a communication audit, including readability studies or readership surveys.

The two-way asymmetric model represents a more modern form of public relations. Here, communication takes on a two-way flow, with the organization sending messages to its publics, as well as receiving feedback from those publics. The ultimate purpose of such communication is best described as "scientific persuasion"—since it employs tested, social science methods to increase the persuasiveness of its communication efforts. Thus, research plays a central role in the two-way asymmetric model. It is used to monitor the attitudes, beliefs, and actions of an organization's publics. More important, it is used to determine the effectiveness of an organization's PR efforts in shaping attitudes.

The two-way symmetric model is quite similar to the previous model, except that its goal is mutual understanding rather than scientific persuasion. Research, therefore, plays a somewhat different role in this model. While it is employed to monitor attitudes and beliefs, the primary reason for conducting research is to determine the level of "mutual understanding" that exists between an organization and its publics. In this sense, the organization and its publics are on equal footing—the "effects" are balanced—unlike the two-way asymmetric model.

The reliability and validity of measures of these models have been established through a number of recent investigations (Carmines & Zeller, 1979; Fabiszak, 1985; Grunig, 1984; Lauzen, 1986; McMillan, 1984; E. Pollack, 1984; R. Pollack, 1986; Schneider, 1985b; Stamm, 1981; Wimmer & Dominick, 1983).

The models identified by Grunig (1984) represent the behaviors of the PR subsystem, the outputs if you will. Grunig and Grunig (1986) and others in a long-term program of research at the University of Maryland have attempted to identify the forces that influence or explain these PR behaviors.

Grunig (1976) initially examined the link between organizational type and PR behavior. He employed a dichotomous typology based upon a mechanical and organic distinction between organizational types (Burns & Stalker, 1961). Grunig defined the mechanical organization as fatalistic since it employed routine, one-way communication, and the organic as problem solving, since it employed a more balanced, adaptive two-way communication style. Unfortunately, he found only a weak relationship between these organizational types and PR behavior.

Jerald Hage and F. Hull (1981) recently expanded this dichotomous typology into four kinds of organizations. They identified the dimension of scale and complexity of the organization. *Scale* refers to the size of the organization, as well as the size and repetitiveness of demand for the organization's products and services. *Complexity* refers to the complexity of knowledge required to produce the organization's products and services. Greater complexity requires more specialists, Hage and Hull (1981) maintain.

A number of studies have tested the relationship between this organizational conceptualization and the PR models (Fabiszak, 1985;

Grunig, 1984; McMillan, 1984; E. Pollack, 1984; R. Pollack, 1986; Schneider, 1985a). The results from these studies are somewhat inconclusive, with only Schneider (1985a) finding any statistically significant support.

Schneider (1985b) subsequently tested the relationship using a "global" level of analysis (Pavlik & Salmon, 1984) in addition to the traditional "individual" level. The individual level uses measures of characteristics of individual practitioners, while the global approach measures characteristics of the PR subsystem as a whole.

The individual level measures "as in previous studies," did not correlate significantly or meaningfully with the models of public relations. The global measures, however, did provide some modest support. For example, the Hage and Hull (1981) traditional organization (i.e., low complexity and small scale) is modestly related to the press agentry model, as expected. The mixed mechanical/organic organization (i.e., high complexity and large scale) is slightly related to the two-way symmetrical model.

Grunig and Grunig (1986) conclude that these fairly inconsistent results indicate a continuing need to search for better explanatory variables to predict the PR models.

One fruitful line has involved an examination of the role of public relations in the dominant coalition (primary policy-making group) of the organization. Involvement in the dominant coalition reflects the influence of the PR department in organizational decision making, authority level of the PR department, top-management support, and so on. Maryland graduate student Ruth A. Pollack (1986) found significant positive correlations between these dominant coalition factors and the PR models. Her survey data indicate a modest positive correlation between representation in the dominant coalition and the two-way asymmetrical model. This factor is negatively related to the press agentry and public information models, and only slightly related to the two-way symmetrical model.

Pollack's data also show significant positive correlations between the educational level of the PR practitioner, years of experience of the PR director, and representation in the dominant coalition. "These correlations suggest that more knowledgeable, experienced practitioners and more sophisticated departments are more likely to be represented in the dominant coalition" (Grunig & Grunig, 1986). Grunig and Grunig also suggest that the PR models may be used situationally. In her master's thesis at Maryland, Rae L. Cupp (1985) found support for this idea in an analysis of case studies of nine chemical companies in West Virginia. Her evidence indicates that an organization may use various models of public relations—depending on the situation or type of problem. In terms of system theory, as the environment changes, the organization uses a different behavior as an adaptive mechanism.

PR Roles

Academic researcher Lalit Acharya's (1985) research similarly suggests that the role of public relations may vary depending upon certain environmental forces. Using Broom and Smith's (1979) PR roles conceptualization, Achayra's study shows that "communication technicians" dominate in organizations with relatively stable, nonthreatening environments. "Communication-process facilitators" dominate in organizations with unstable, yet low-threat environments. "Expert-prescribers" tend to dominate in organizations with unstable, threatening environments—which allow little time for environmental scanning (Broom, 1986; Dozier, 1986). Finally, "problem-solving process facilitators" function in stable, yet high-threat environments.

Broom (1986) presents evidence that in some situations, PR behaviors may be more accurately represented by a closed rather than an open system model.

An open systems model of public relations suggests purposive role-taking and activities based on a priori and specific knowledge of an organization's situation and environment. . . . The more historically accurate portrayal, however, would show routine and institutionalized public relations responses (to an organization's environment) that are unsystematically related to organizational survival and growth, or demise. (Broom, 1986)

CONCLUSION

In conclusion, recent research suggests that general system theory may provide a useful perspective—or paradigm—for understanding the function of public relations in organizations. Perhaps more important, it also suggests that this is only a beginning. Continued research is needed to enrich our basic understanding of all aspects of public relations and to help this field achieve full professional status.

REFERENCES

Acharya, L. (1985). Public relations environments. *Journalism Quarterly, 62,* 577-584.

Aiello, R. J. (1983). Employee attitude surveys: Impact on corporate decisions. *Public Relations Journal, 7*(1), 21.

Albritton, R., & Manheim, J. B. (1983). News of Rhodesia: The impact of a PR campaign. *Journalism Quarterly, 60,* 622-628.

Allen, C. T., & Weber, J. D. (1983). How presidential media use affects individuals' beliefs about conservation. *Journalism Quarterly, 60,* 98-107.

Anderson, R. B. (1986). *The role of self-efficacy theory in the design of campaigns to prevent drunken driving: A social marketing approach.* Paper presented at the meeting of the Association for Education in Journalism and Mass Communication, Norman, OK.

Armstrong, R. A. (1981). The concept and practice of issues management in the United States. *Vital Speeches,* October 1.

Aronoff, C. E. (1975). Newspapermen and practitioners differ widely on PR role. *Public Relations Journal, 31*(8), 24-25.

Aronoff, C. E. (1976). Predictors of success in placing releases in newspapers. *Journalism Quarterly, 53*(4), 43-57.

Asch, S. (1958). Effects of group pressure upon the modification and distortion of judgments. In E. E. Maccoby, T. M. Newcomb, & E. L. Hartley (Eds.), *Readings in social psychology* (3rd. ed., pp.174-183). New York: Holt, Rinehart.

Atwood, R., & Dervin, B. (1981). *Challenges to social-cultural predictors of information-seeking: A test of race vs. situation movement state.* Paper presented at the meeting of the International Communication Association, Minneapolis, MN.

Atwood, L. E., Sohn, A. B., & Sohn, H. (1978). Daily newspaper Contributions to community discussion. *Journalism Quarterly, 55*(3), 570-576.

Baker, M. S., Jr. (1977). The image makers image. *Public Relations Journal 33*(8), 18-19.

Barlow, W., & Kaufmann, C. (1975). Public relations and economic literacy. *Public Relations Review, 1*(2), 14-22.

Bauer, R. A. (1964). The obstinate audience: The influence process from the point of view of social communication. *American Psychologist, 19,* 319-328.

Baxter, B. (1985). Education for corporate. *Public Relations Review, 11*(1), 38-41.

Beardsley, J. (1986). Interview.

Benton, M., & Frazier, G. (1976). The agenda-setting function of the mass media at three levels of information-holding. *Communication Research, 3,* 261-274.

Berelson, B., Lazarsfeld, P. F., & McPhee, W. (1954). *Voting.* Chicago: University of Chicago Press.

Bernays, E. L. (1923). *Crystallizing public opinion.* New York: Boni and Liveright.

Bernays, E. L. (1937). Recent trends in public relations activities. *Public Opinion Quarterly, 1*(1), 147-151.

Bernays, E. L. (1955). *The engineering of consent*. Norman: University of Oklahoma Press.

Bernays, E. L. (1986). Interview.

Bertalanffy, L. von. (1968). *General system theory*. New York: G. Braziller.

Beyer, C. (1986). Salaries. *Public Relations Journal, 42*(6), 26.

Bird, S. E. (1985). Content of television political spot ads for female candidates. *Journalism Quarterly, 62*(2), 278-283.

Bishop, R. L., & Bosworth, A. M., IV. (1986). *Correlates of prestige and success in public relations*. Unpublished manuscript.

Bissland, J. II.(1986). *The effort to upgrade public relations evaluation practices: What the record shows*. Unpublished manuscript.

Blake, D. H., & Toros, V. (1976). The global image makers. *Public Relations Journal, 32*(6), 10-13.

Boorstin, D. (1964). *The image: A guide to pseudo-events in America*. New York: Harper & Row.

Breed, W. (1955) Social control in the newsroom. *Social Forces, 33*, 326-335.

Brody, E. W. (1984). Antipathy between public relations, journalism exaggerated. *Public Relations Review, 10*(4), 11-15.

Brody, E. W. (1985). Changing role and requirements of public relations. *Public Relations Review, 11*(4), 22-28.

Broom, G. M. (1977). Coorientational measurement of public issues. *Public Relations Review, 3*(4), 110-128.

Broom, G. M. (1982). Comparison of sex roles in public relations. *Public Relations Review, 8*(3), 17-22.

Broom, G. M. (1986). *Public relations roles and systems theory: Functional and historicist causal models*. Paper presented at the meeting of the International Communication Association, Chicago.

Broom, G. M., & Dozier, D. (1985). *Determinants and consequences of public relations roles*. Paper presented at the meeting of the Association for Education in Journalism and Mass Communication, Memphis, TN.

Broom, G. M., & Dozier, D. (1986). Advancement for public relations role models. *Public Relations Review, 12*(1), 47.

Broom, G. M., Ferguson-DeThorne, M.A., Ruksza, A.M. (1980). Case study effects on student opinions of big business. *Public Relations Review, 61*(2), 50-57.

Broom, G. M., & Smith, G. D. (1979). Testing the practitioner's impact on clients. *Public Relations Review, 5*(3), 47-59.

Burns, T., & Stalker, G. M. (1961). *The management of innovation*. London: Tavistock.

Burger, C. (1981). Management's view of the future of public relations. *Public Relations Review, 7*(2), 3-12.

Cain, R. L., Katz, E., & Rosenthal, D. B. (1969). *The politics of community conflict: The floridation decision*. New York: Bobbs-Merrill.

Cantor, B. (1984). 1984 the year ahead. *Public Relations Journal, 40*(1), 12-15.

Carmines, E. G., & Zeller, R. A. (1979). *Quantitative applications in the social sciences. Vol. 17: Reliability and validity assessment*. Newbury Park, CA: Sage.

Carter, R. E., & Mitovsky, W. J. (1961). Actual and perceived distances in the news. *Journalism Quarterly, 38*(2), 223-225.

Cartwright, D. (1949). Some principles of mass communication: Selected findings of research on the sale of United States War Bonds. *Human Relations, 11*(3), 253-267.

Center, A. (1977). Canvassing the calling. *Public Relations Journal, 33*(11), 40-41, 46.

Center, A., & Walsh, F. E. (1985). *Public relations practices: Managerial case studies and problems* (3rd ed.). Englewood Cliffs, NJ: Prentice-Hall.

Chaffee, S. T., & Hochheimer, J. L. (1985). The beginnings of political communication research in the United States: Origins of the "limited effects model." In M. Gurevitch & M. P. Levy (Eds.), *Mass communication review yearbook* (Vol. 5, pp. 75-104). Newbury Park, CA: Sage.

Chaffee, S. T., & Wilson, D. G. (1977). Media rich, media poor: Two studies in diversity in agenda holding. *Journalism Quarterly, 54*(3), 466-476.

Chase, W. H. (1975). How companies are using corporate advertising. *Public Relations Journal, 31*(11), 26.

Clavier, D. E., & Kalupa, F. B. (1983). Corporate rebuttals to "Trial by television." *Public Relations Review, 9*(1), 24-36.

Clavier, D. E., & Wright, D. K. (1982). Educators and professional organizations. *Public Relations Review, 8*(2), 25-30.

Cline, C. (1982). Image of public relations in mass communication texts. *Public Relations Review, 8*(3), 63-72.

Cline, C. G., & Masel-Waters, L. (1984). Backlash: The impact of a video case study on opinions of AT&T. *Public Relations Review, 10*(3), 39-46.

Cline, C. G., Toth, E. L., Turk, J. V., Waters, L. M., Johnson, N., & Stith, H. (1986). *The velvet ghetto: The impact of the increasing percentage of women in public relations and business communication.* San Francisco: International Communication Association.

Coch, L., & French, J. R. P., Jr.(1948). Overcoming resistance to change. *Human Relations, 1,* 512-532.

Cohen, B. C. (1963). *The press ANd foreign policy.* Princeton, NJ: Princeton University Press.

Cohen, D. (1975). *A report on a non-election agenda-setting study.* Paper presented at the meeting of the Association for Education in Journalism, Ottawa, Canada.

Commission on Public Relations Education. (1975). Design for public relations education. Public Relations Division, Association for Education in Journalism, and Public Relations Society of America.

Comstock, G., Chaffee, S., Katzman, N., McCombs, M., & Roberts, D. (1978). *Television and human behavior.* New York: Columbia University Press.

Culbertson, H. M. (1983). How public relations textbooks handle honesty and lying. *Public Relations Review, 9*(2), 65-73.

Culbertson, H. M. (1985). Practitioner roles: Their meaning for educators. *Public Relations Review, 11*(4), 5-21.

Culbertson, H. M., & STEMPEL, G. H., III. (1985). Linking beliefs and public relations efforts. *Public Relations Research and Education, 2*(2), 23-35.

Cupp, R. L. (1985). *A study of public relations crisis management in West Virginia chemical companies.* Master's thesis, University of Maryland, College Park.

Darling, H. L. (1975). How companies are using corporate advertising. *Public Relations Journal, 31*(11), 26-29.

Davison, W. P. (1982). The third-person effect of communication. *Public Opinion Quarterly, 46,* 1-15.

DeBock, H. (1976). Influence of in-state election poll reports on candidate preference in 1972. *Journalism Quarterly, 53*(3), 457-462.

DeBock, H. (1980). Gratification frustration during a newspaper strike and a television blackout. *Journalism Quarterly, 57*(1), 61-66.

Denbow, C. H., & Culbertson, H. M. (1985). Linkage beliefs and diagnosing an image. *Public Relations Review, 11*(1), 29-37.

Dervin, B. (1980). *Information as a user construct: The relevance of perceived information needs to synthesis and interpretation.* Paper presented at the meeting of the Research and Educational Practice Unit, National Institute for Education, Washington, DC.

Dervin, B. (1981). Mass communicating: Changing conceptions of the audience. In R. E. Rice & W. J. Paisely (Eds.), *Public communication campaigns* (pp. 71-81). Newbury Park, CA: Sage.

Dewey, J. (1927). *The public and its problems.* Chicago: Swallow Press.

Dewey, J. (1938). *Logic: The theory of inquiry.* New York: Holt, Rinehart & Winston.

Donohue, G. A., Olien, C. N., & Tichenor, P. J. (1973). Mass media functions, knowledge and social control. *Journalism Quarterly, 50,* 652-659.

Donohue, G. A., Olien, C. N., & Tichenor, P. J. (1974). Communities, pollution, and fight for survival. Journal of Environmental Education, 6(3), 29-37.

Donohue, G. A., Olien, C. N., & Tichenor, P.J. (1985a). Leader and editor views of role of press in community development. *Journalism Quarterly, 62*(2), 367-372.

Donohue, G. A., Olien, C. N., & Tichenor, P. J. (1985b). Reporting conflict by pluralism, newspaper type and ownership. *Journalism Quarterly, 62*(3), 489-499.

Doolittle, J. C. (1979). News media use by older adults. *Journalism Quarterly, 56*(2), 311-317.

Dozier, D. M. (1984). Program evaluation and the roles of practitioners. *Public Relations Review, 10*(2), 13-21.

Dozier, D. (1986). *The environmental scanning function of public relations practitioners and participation in management decision making.* Paper presented at the meeting of the Association for Education in Journalism and Mass Communication, Norman, OK.

Druck, K. B., & Hiebert, R. (1979). *Your personal guidebook to help you chart a more successful career in public relations.* New York: Public Relations Society of America.

Dunwoody, S., & Ryan, M. (1983). Public information persons as mediators between scientists and journalists. *Journalism Quarterly, 60*(4), 647-656.

Ehling, W. P. (1984). Application of decision theory in the construction of a theory of public relations management I. *Public Relations Research & Education, 1*(2), 25-38.

Ehling, W. P. & Hesse, M. B. (1983). Use of "issue management" in public relations. *Public Relations Review, 9*(2), 18-36.

Einseidel, E. F., Salamone, K. L., Schneider, F. P. (1984) Crime: Effects of media exposure and personal experience on issue salience. *Journalism Quarterly, 61*(1), 131-136.

Ettema, J. S., Brown, J. W., Leupker, R. V. (1983). Knowledge-gap effects in a health information campaign. *Public Opinion Quarterly, 47*(4), 516-527.

Evans, F. J. (1984). Business and the press: Conflicts over roles, fairness. *Public Relations Review, 10*(4), 33-42.

Fabiszak, D. L. (1985). *Public relations in hospitals: Testing the Grunig theory of organizations, environments and models of public relations.* Master's thesis, University of Maryland, College Park, MD.

Fay, T. J. (1984). Corporate advertising. In B. Cantor & C. Burger (Eds.), *Experts in action: Inside public relations* (pp. 159-174). New York: Longman.

Ferguson-DeThorne, M. A. (1978). Energy conservation treatment in Exxon's "The Lamp." *Public Relations Review, 4*(1), 43-57.

Festinger, A. (1957). *A theory of cognitive dissonance.* Stanford, CA: Stanford University Press.

Finn, D. (1981). *The business-media relationship: Countering misconception and distrust, an AMA research study.* New York: AMACOM, a division of American Management Association.

Finn, P. (1982). Demystifying public relations. *Public Relations Journal 38*(5), 12-17.

Flay, B. R. (1981). On improving the chances of mass media health promotion programs causing meaningful changes in behavior. In M. Meyer (Ed.), *Health education by television and radio* (pp. 56-91). Munich, Germany: K. G. Saur Verlag KG.

Franzen, R. S. (1977). An NBS internal communications study: A comment. *Public Relations Review, 3*(4), 83-95.

Garbett, T. F. (1981). *Corporate advertising: The what, the why and the how.* New York: McGraw-Hill.

Garramone, G. M. (1984a). Voter responses to negative political ads. *Journalism Quarterly, 61*(2), 250-259.

Garramone, G. M. (1984b). Motivation models: Replication across media for political campaign content. *Journalism Quarterly, 61*(3), 537-541.

Garramone, G. M. (1985). Motivation and selective attention to political information formats. *Journalism Quarterly, 62*(1), 37-44.

Gaziano, C. (1984). Neighborhood newspapers, citizen groups and public affairs knowledge gaps. *Journalism Quarterly, 61*(3), 556-566.

Gilberg, S., Eyal, C., McCombs, M., & Nicholas, D. (1980). The State of the Union Address and the press agenda. *Journalism Quarterly, 57*(4), 584-588.

Gilsdorf, J. W., & Vawter, L. K. (1983). Public relations professionals rate their associations. *Public Relations Review, 9*(4), 26-40.

Gitter, A. G. (1981). Public relations roles: Press agent or counselor? *Public Relations Review, 7*(3), 35-41.

Glenn, M. C., Gruber, W. H., Rabin, K. H. (1982). Using computers in corporate public affairs. *Public Relations Review, 8*(3), 34-42.

Goodman, R. I. (1981). Selecting public service announcements for television. *Public Relations Review, 7*(3), 25-34.

Goodman, R., & Ruch, R. S. (1982). The role of research in internal communications. *Public Relations Journal, 38*(7), 16-19.

Gorney, S. (1975). Status of women in public relations. *Public Relations Journal, 31*(5), 10-13.

Gorney, C. (1985). Steel shutdown in Lackawanna: A case study. *Public Relations Quarterly, 30*(2), 20-26.

Graff, L. (1981). The three phenomena of public relations. *Public Relations Journal, 7*(1), 17-26.

Grass, R. C. (1977). Measuring the effects of corporate advertising. *Public Relations Review, 3*(4), 39-50.

Grunig, J. E. (1976). Communication behaviors occurring in decision and nondecision situations. *Public Relations Review, 2*(2), 252-263.

Grunig, J. E. (1977). Evaluating employee communications in research operation. *Public Relations Review, 3*(4), 61-82.

Grunig, J. E. (1978). Defining publics in public relations: The case of a suburban hospital. *Journalism Quarterly, 55*(1), 109-118.

Grunig, J. E. (1979a). Time budgets, level of involvement and use of the mass media. *Journalism Quarterly, 56*(2), 248-261.

Grunig, J. E. (1979b). Special section: The two worlds of public relations research. *Public Relations Review, 5,* 11.

Grunig, J. E. (1982). Developing economic education programs for the press. *Public Relations Review, 8*(3), 43-62.

Grunig, J. E. (1983a). Communication behaviors and attitudes of environmental publics: Two studies. *Journalism Monographs, 81.*

Grunig, J. E. (1983b). Basic research provides knowledge that makes evaluation possible. *Public Relations Quarterly, 28*(3): 28-32.

Grunig, J. E. (1983c). Washington reporter publics of corporate public affairs programs. *Journalism Quarterly, 39*(4), 603-614.

Grunig, J. E. (1984). Organizations, environments, and models of public relations. *Public Relations Research and Education, 1*(4), 6-29.

Grunig, L. S. (1985). *A structural reconceptualization of the organizational communication audit, with applicattion to a state department of education.* Paper presented at the meeting of the International Communication Association, Honolulu.

Grunig, J. E. (1986). Interview.

Grunig, J. E., Dozier, D. M., Ehling, W. P., Grunig, L. S., Repper, F. C., & White, J. (1985). *In search of excellence in public relations and communication management.* Grant proposal submitted to the International Association of Business Communicators Foundation.

Grunig. J. E., & Grunig, L. S. (1986). *Application of open systems theory to public relations: Review of a program of research.* Paper presented at the meeting of the International Communication Association, Chicago.

Grunig, J. E., & Hickson, R. H. (1976). An evaluation of academic research in public relations. *Public Relations Review, 2*(1), 31-43.

Grunig, J. E., & Hunt, T. (1984). *Managing public relations.* New York: Holt, Rinehart & Winston.

Grunig, J. E., & Ipes, D. A. (1983). The anatomy of a campaign against drunken driving. *Public Relations Review, 9*(2), 36-52.

Grunig, J. E., & Stamm, K. R. (1979). Cognitive strategies and the resolution of environmental issues: A second study. Journalism Quarterly, 56(4), 715-726.

Haefner, J. F. (1976). Can TV advertising influence employers to hire or train disadvantaged persons? *Journalism Quarterly, 53*(2), 211-215.

Hage, J. (1980). *Theories of organizations.* New York: John Wiley.

Hage, J., & Hull, F. (1981). *A typology of environmental niches based on knowledge technology and scale: The implications for innovation and productivity* (Working Paper 1). College Park: University of Maryland, Center for the Study of Innovation, Entrepreneurship, and Organization Strategy.

Hale, F. D. (1978). Press releases vs. newspaper coverage of California Supreme Court Decisions. *Journalism Quarterly, 55*(4), 696-702.

Hamilton, S. C. (1986). *A schema for analyzing the imaginative component in public relations.* Paper presented at the meeting of the Association for Education in Journalism and Mass Communication, Norman, OK.

Harper, J., & Danielson, W. (1986). *The newspaper management game.* Austin, TX: Wayne Danielson Software.

Harris, A., Garramone, G., Pizante, G., & Komiza, M. (1985). Computers in constituent communication. *Public Relations Review, 11*(3), 34-39.

Haskins, R. L. (1984). Annual reports I: Difficult reading and getting more so. *Public Relations Review, 10*(2), 49-55.

Haskins, R. L. (1981). Public relations opportunities in two-year colleges. *Public Relations Review, 7*(3), 42-52.

Hawkins, K. (1984). Cable: A need to get beyond awareness. *Public Relations Journal, 40*(1), 33.

Heath, R. L., & Phelps, G. (1984). Annual reports II: Readability of reports vs. business press. *Public Relations Review, 10*(2), 56-62.

Hesse, M. B. (1981). Strategies of the political communication process. *Public Relations Review, 7*(1), 32-47.

Hiebert, R. E., & Devine, C. M. (1985). Government research and evaluation gap. *Public Relations Review, 11*(3), 47-56.

Hochheimer, J. L. (1982). "Probing the Foundations of Political Communication in Campaigns: The Dispersion Process of Media." Paper presented at the International Communication Association, Boston.

Hofstetter, C. R., Zirkin, C., & Bass, T. F. (1978). Political imagery and information in an age of television. *Journalism Quarterly, 55*(3), 562-569.

Holsti, O. R. (1968). Content analysis. In G. Lindzeyf & E. Aronson (Eds.), *The handbook of social psychology: Research methods* (Vol. 2, pp.596-692). Cambridge, MA: Addison-Wesley.

Hovland, C. I., Janis, I. L., & Kelley, H. H. (1953). *Communication and persuasion.* New Haven, CT: Yale University Press.

Hovland, C. I., Lumsdaine, A. A., & Sheffield, F. D. (1949). *Experiments on mass communication.* Princeton, NJ: Princeton University Press.

Hunt, T. (1985). *Instructional simulations help PR students understand roles in organizational communication.* Paper presented at the the meeting of the Association for Education in Journalism and Mass Communication, Memphis, TN.

Hurd, R. E., & Singletary, M. W. (1984). Newspaper endorsement influence on the 1980 presidential election vote. *Journalism Quarterly, 61*(2), 332-338.

Hyman, H. M., & Sheatsley, P. B. (1947). Some reasons why information campaigns fail. *Public Opinion Quarterly, 11,* 412-423.

Hynds, E. C. (1980). Business coverage is getting better. *Journalism Quarterly. 57*(2), 297-304.

Izard, R. S. (1985). Public confidence in the news media. *Journalism Quarterly, 62*(2). 247-256.

Jaffe, J. (1983). Interview.

Jaspers, E., & Gitter, A. G. (1982). Are public relations graduate students learning what they should be? *Public Relations Quarterly, 27*(2), 13.

Jeffers, D. W. (1977). Performance expectations as a measure of relative status of news and public relations people. *Journalism Quarterly, 54*(2), 299-306.

Jeffers, D. W. (1983). Discovering media-value associations. *Public Relations Review, 9*(1), 37-44.

Jeffers, D. W., & Bateman, D. N. (1980). Redefining the role of the company magazine. *Public Relations Review, 6*(2), 11-29.

Jeffres, L. (1975). Functions of media behaviors. *Communication Research, 2,* 136-162.

Johnson, T. B., & Rabin, K. (1977). Public relations faculty: What are their qualifications. *Public Relations Review, 3*(1), 38-48.

Jones, J. F. (1975). Audit: A new tool for public relations. *Public Relations Journal, 31*(7), 6-8.

Joseph, T. (1985-1986). The women are coming, the women are coming. *Public Relations Quarterly, 30*(4), 21.

Joslyn, R. A. (1980). The content of political spot ads. *Journalism Quarterly, 57*(1), 92-98.

Judd, L. R. (1986). *Can public relations practitioners predict attitudes?* Paper presented at the meeting of the International Communication Association, Chicago.

Kalupa, F. B., & Allen, T. H. (1982). Future directions in public relations education. *Public Relations Review, 8*(2), 31-45.

Kalupa, F. B.. & Bateman, J. C. (1980). Accrediting public relations education. *Public Relations Review, 6*(1), 18-39.

Kalupa, F. B., & Sievers, C. G. (1986). *Public relations licensure: Practitioner and educator attitudes.* Paper presented at the meeting of the Association for Education in Journalism and Mass Communication, Norman, OK.

Kendall, R. (1980). Internship practices in public relations. *Public Relations Review, 6*(2), 30-37.

Kendall, R. (1984a). Public relations faculty: Costs and compensation. *Public Relations Review, 10*(1), 44-52.

Kendall, R. (1984b). Public relations employment: Huge growth projected. *Public Relations Review, 10*(3), 13-26.

Kendall, R., & Anderson, J. W. (1985-1986) *Educating for public relations: A national survey of topics "essential" to the PR curriculum.* Report for the Commission on Undergraduate Public Relations Education.

Kirban, L. (1983). Showing what we do makes a difference. *Public Relations Quarterly, 38*(3), 22-27.

Klapper, J. T. (1960). *The effects of mass communication.* Glencoe, IL: Free Press.

Kline, F. G., & Ettema, J. E. (1977). Deficits, differences, and ceilings: Contingent conditions for understanding the knowledge gap. *Communication Research, 4*(2), 179-202.

Kopenhaver, L. L. (1985). Aligning values of practitioners and journalists. *Public Relations Review, 11*(2), 34-42.

Kopenhaver, L. L., Martinson, D. L., & Ryan, M. (1984). How public relations practitioners and editors in Florida view each other. *Journalism Quarterly, 61*(4). 860-865.

Krippendorff, K., & Eleey, M. F. (1986). Monitoring a group's symbolic environment. *Public Relations Review, 12*(1), 13-36.

Krugman, H. E. (1965). The impact of television: Learning without involvement. *Public Opinion Quarterly, 29,* 349-356.

Kuhn, T. (1970). *The structure of scientific revolutions.* Chicago: University of Chicago Press.

Lang, G. E., & Lang, K. (1983). *The battle for public opinion.* New York: Columbia University Press.

Larson, M. A., & Massetti-Miller, K. L. (1984). Measuring change after a public education campaign. *Public Relations Review, 10*(4), 23-32.

Latshaw, W. A. (1977). Target group research: New tool for advocacy advertising. *Public Relations Journal, 33*(11), 28-33.

Lasswell, H. D. (1972). The structure of communication in society. In W. Schramm & D. F. Roberts (Eds.), *The process and effects of mass communication* (pp. 84-99). Urbana: University of Illinois Press.

Lauzen, M. (1986). *Public relations in conflict with the franchise system.* Doctoral dissertation, University of Maryland, College Park.

Lazarsfeld, P. F. (1959). Problems in methodology. In R. K. Merton, L. Broon, & L. S. Cottrell (Eds.), *Sociology today: Problems and prospects* (pp. 39-78). New York: Basic Books.

Lazarsfeld, P. F., Berelson, B., & Gaudet, H. (1944). *The people's choice.* New York: Duell, Sloan & Pearce.

Leahigh, A. K. (1985-1986). If you can't count it, does it count? *Public Relations Quarterly, 30*(4), 23.

Leffingwell, R. J. (1980). The communication gap between social science and practitioners. *Public Relations Quarterly, 25*(1), 29.

Leffingwell, R. J. (1981-1982). Establishing a dialogue—bridging PR practitioner-social scientist communication gap. *Public Relations Quarterly, 26*(4), 30.

Lehrman, C. K. (1985a). Salary survey. *Public Relations Journal, 41*(6), 26.

Lehrman, C. K. (1985b). The buying habits of PR professionals. *Public Relations Journal, 41*(8), 19-22.

Lemert, J. B., Mitzman, B. N., Seither, M. A., Cook, R. H., & Hackett, R. (1977). Journalists and mobilizing information. *Journalism Quarterly, 54*(4), 721-726.

Lerbinger, O. (1977). Corporate uses of research in public relations. *Public Relations Review, 3*(4), 11-19.

Levey, M. R., & Windahl, S. (1984). Audience activity and gratifications: A conceptual clarification and exploration. *Communication Research, 7*(1), 51-78.

Lindenmann, W. K. (1980). Use of community case studies on opinion research. *Public Relations Review, 6*(1), 40-50.

Lippmann, W. (1921). *Public opinion.* New York: Macmillan.

Lorz, F. M. (1984). Focus group research in a winning campaign. *Public Relations Review, 10*(2), 28-38.

Lumby, M. E. (1980). Using classified ads to find a job in public relations. *Public Relations Review, 6*(3), 33-39.

Luttbeg, N. R. (1983). Proximity does not assure newsworthiness. *Journalism Quarterly, 60*(4), 731-732.

Lynn, J. R., Wyatt, R. O., Gaines, J., Pearce, R., & Vanden Bergh, B. (1978). How source affects response to public service advertising. *Journalism Quarterly, 55*(4), 716-720.

Mahon, W. (1986). *A study of the media attention given to the state's five largest public research universities in four large circulation newspapers in Pennsylvania.* Report for the Office of Public Information, Pennsylvania State University.

Marker, R. K. (1977). The Armstrong/PR data measurement system. *Public Relations Review, 3*(4), 51-60.

McCleneghan, J. S. (1980). Media and non-media effects in Texas mayoral elections. *Journalism Quarterly, 57*(1), 129-134.

McCombs, M. (1974). *A comparison of intrapersonal and interpersonal agendas of public issues.* Paper presented at the meeting of the International Communication Association, New Orleans, LA.

McCombs, M. (1977). Agenda-setting function of mass media. *Public Relations Review 3*(4), 89-95.

McCombs, M., & Schulte, H. (1975). *The expanding domain of the agenda-setting function of mass communication.* Paper presented at the meeting of the World Association for Public Opinion Research, Montreaux, Switzerland.

McDonald, D. G., & Glynn, C. J. (1984). The stability of media gratifications. *Journalism Quarterly, 61*(3), 542-549.

McElreath, M. P. (1977). Public relations evaluative research: Summary statement. *Public Relations Review, 3*(4), 129-136.

McGuire, W. J. (1969). The nature of attitudes and attitude change. In G. Lindzey & E. Aronson (Eds.), *Handbook of social psychology: The individual in a social context* (Vol. 3, 2nd ed., pp. 136-314). Cambridge, MA: Addison-Wesley.

McGuire, W. J. (1972). Attitude change: The information-processing paradigm. In C. G. McClintock (Ed.), *Experimental social psychology* (pp. 108-141). New York: Holt, Rinehart, & Winston.

McGuire, W. J. (1981). Theoretical foundations of campaigns. In R. E. Rice & W. J. Paisley (Eds.), *Public communication campaigns* (pp. 41-70). Newbury Park, CA: Sage.

McCleod, J. M., & Chaffee, S. H. (1973). Interpersonal approaches to communication research. In S. H. Chaffee & J. M. McCleod (Eds.), Interpersonal perception and communication [Special issue]. *American Behavioral Scientist, 16*(1), 483-488.

McMillan, S. J. (1984). *Public relations in trade and professional associations: Location, model, structure, environment and values.* Master's thesis, University of Maryland, College Park.

Mendelsohn, H. (1973). Some reasons why information campaigns can succeed. *Public Opinion Quarterly, 37*(1), 50-61.

Miller, M. W. (1982). Corporate public relations update. *Public Relations Journal, 38*(1), 21-24.

Morgan, B., & Schiemann, W. (1983). Why internal communication is failing. *Public Relations Journal, 39*(3), 15-17.

Morrissey, J. A. (1978). Will the real public relations professional please stand up? *Public Relations Journal, 34*(12), 24-27.

Morton, L. P. (1985). Use of photos in public relations messages: Public relations messages. *Public Relations Review, 11*(4), 16-22.

Moyers, B. (1983). *A walk through the 20th century with Bill Moyers: The imagemakers.* Videotape produced by Public Television.

Mulder, R. (1979). The effects of televised political ads in the 1975 Chicago mayoral election. *Journalism Quarterly, 56*(2), 336-340.

Nachmias, D., & Nachmias, C. (1976). *Research methods in the social sciences.* New York: St. Martin's Press.

Nadler, M. K. (1986). *An exploration of the feminization of public relations.* Paper presented at the meeting of the International Communication Association, Chicago.

Nager, N. R., & Allen, T. H. (1984). *Public relations management by objectives.* New York: Longman.

Naples, M. J. (1979). Effective frequency: The relationship between frequency and advertising effectiveness. New York: Association of National Advertisers.

Nayman, O., McKee, B. K., & Lattimore, D. L. (1977). Public relations personnel and print journalists: A comparison of professionalism. *Journalism Quarterly, 54*(3), 492-497.

Netteburg, K. (1984). Evaluating change: A church publication studies its readers. *Public Relations Review, 10*(2), 63-71.

Newsom, D. A. (1983). Conflict: Who gets media attention and why? *Public Relations Review, 9*(3), 35-39.

Nickerson, O. O., Schuster, F. E., & Murdick, R. G. (1982). Touting your human resource management. *Public Relations Journal, 38*(8), 32-33.

Nord, D. P. (1981). The politics of agenda setting in late 19th century cities. *Journalism Review, 7*(4), 565-574.

Norris, V. P. (1982). Consumer magazine prices and the mythical advertising subsidy. *Journalism Quarterly, 59*(2), 205-211.

Norris, V. P. (1983). Toward a "social control" in the advertising agency. *Journal of Advertising, 12*(1), 30-33.

Norris, V. P. (1984). Mad economics: An analysis of an adless magazine. *Journal of Communication, 34*(1), 44-61.

Oates, W. R. (1985). *Computer-based persuasion: Teaching a new medium for PR communication.* Paper presented at the meeting of the Association for Education in Journalism and Mass Communication, Memphis, TN.

O'Brien, A. (1980). Public relations of anti-stereotype television spots. *Public Relations Review, 6*(3), 14-22.

O'Keefe, G., & Reid-Nash, K. (1986). *Uses and effects of public service announcements.* Report: National Participation in Drug and Alcohol Abuse, Washington, DC.

Olasky, M. N. (1984). Retrospective: Bernays' doctrine of public opinion. *Public Relations Review, 10*(3), 3-12.

Olien, C. N., Donohue, D. A., & Tichenor, P. J. (1978). Community structure and media use. *Journalism Quarterly, 55*(3), 445-455.

Ostrom, T. M. (1969). The relationship between the affective, behavioral, and cognitive components of attitude. *Journal of Experimental Social Psychology, 5,* 12-30.

Park, R. E. (1923). The natural history of the newspaper. *American Journal of Sociology, 29,* 273-289.

Patterson, T. E., & McClure, R. D. (1976). *The unseeing eye: The myth of television power in national politics.* New York: Putnam.

Patti, C. H., & McDonald, J. P. (1985). Corporate advertising: Processes, practices, and perspectives (1970-1989). *Journal of Advertising, 14*(1), 42-49.

Pavlik, J. V. (1987). Simulator: A pilot interactive simulation program for use in teaching public relations. *Public Relations Research and Education* (in press).

Pavlik, J. V., Nwosu, I. E., & Ettel-Gonzalez, D. (1982). Why employees read company newsletters. *Public Relations Review, 8*(3), 23-33.

Pavlik, J. V., & Salmon, C. T. (1984). Theoretic approaches in public relations research. *Public Relations Research and Education, 1*(2), 39-49.

Pavlik, J. V., & Summerall, A. (1986). *A systematic review of public relations research: 1976-1985.* Unpublished manuscript.

Pavlik, J. V., & Wackman, D. (1985). *Cognitive structure and involvement in a health information campaign.* Paper presented at the meeting of the International Communication Association, Honolulu.

Pincus, J. D., & Rayfield, R. (1986). *The relationship between top management communication and organizational effectiveness.* Paper presented at the meeting of the Association for Education in Journalism and Mass Communication, Norman, OK.

Pollack, E. J. (1984). *An organizational analysis of four public relations models in the federal government.* Master's thesis, University of Maryland, College Park.

Pollack, R. A. (1986). *Testing the Grunig organizational theory in scientific organizations: Public relations and the values of the dominant coalition.* Master's thesis, University of Maryland, College Park.

Porter, D. T. (1986). *Contributions of systems theory to the study of communication in organizations: The Santa Claus of organizational communication.* Paper presented at the meeting of the International Communication Association, Chicago.

Proctor, J. (1983). The path to the top. *Public Relations Journal, 39*(6), 25-29.

PR Reporter. (1986). *29*(7).

Public Relations Journal. (1976). The price of institutional advertising in 1975. *32*(11), 28-29.

Public Relations Journal. (1976). How public relations executives shape corporate advertising. *32*(11), 32-33.

Public Relations Journal. (1977). Public relations role in corporate advertising. *33*(1), 34-35.

Public Relations Journal. (1979). Measuring corporate advertising effectiveness. *35*(11), 19-23.

Public Relations Journal. (1982). Public relations education: Two surveys. *38*(2), 19-33.

Public Relations Journal. (1984a). Corporate advertising costs. *40*(11), 20-27.

Public Relations Journal. (1984b). Annual report credibility. *40*(11), 31-34.

Rada, S. E. (1983). Delicate balance: Corporate and agency membership in PRSA. *Public Relations Review, 9*(4), 14-25.

Ray, M. L. (1973). Marketing communication and the hierarchy-of-effects. In P. Clarke (Ed.), *New models for mass communication research* (pp. 47-176). Newbury Park, CA: Sage.

Reagan, J., & Ducey, R. V. (1983). Effects of news measure on selection of state government new source. *Journalism Quarterly, 60*(12), 211-217.

Reeves, B. (1983). Now you see them, now you don't: Demonstrating effects of communication programs. *Public Relations Quarterly, 28*(3), 17-21, 27.

Reeves, B., & Ferguson-DeThorne, M. A. (1980). Measuring the effect of messages about social responsibility. *Public Relations Review, 6*(3), 40-55.

Resnick, A., & Stern, B. L. (1977). An analysis of information content in television advertising. *Journal of Marketing, 41*(1), 50-53.

Rippey, J. N. (1981). Perceptions by selected executives of local business coverage. *Journalism Quarterly, 58*(3), 382-387.

Ris, T. F. (1977). Report card on industry's educational materials. *Public Relations Journal, 33*(6), 8-11.

Robinson, E. J. (1969). *Public relations and survey research* (p. 13). New York: Appleton-Century-Crofts.

Rokeach, M. (1979). *Understanding human values.* New York: Free Press.

Roscho, B. (1975). *Newsmaking.* Chicago: University of Chicago Press.

Rowan, M. (1986). Interview.

Rubin, A. (1985). Whose news is it? *Public Relations Journal, 41*(10), 18-23.

Ryan, M., & Martinson, D. L. (1984). Ethical values, the flow of journalistic information and public relations persons. *Journalism Quarterly, 61*(1), 27-34.

Ryan, M., & Martinson, D. L. (1985). Public relations practitioners, public interest and management. *Journalism Quarterly, 62*(1), 111-115.

Sachs, W. S. (1981). Corporate advertising: ends, means, problems. *Public Relations Journal, 37*(11), 14-17.

Sachs, W. S., & Chasin, J. (1976). The price of institutional advertising in 1975. *Public Relations Journal, 32*(11), 28-29.

Sachs, W. S., & Chasin, J. (1977). How companies evaluate their corporate advertising. *Public Relations Journal, 33*(11), 14-17.

Sachsman, D. B. (1976). Public relations influence on coverage of environment in San Francisco area. *Journalism Quarterly, 53*(1), 54-60.

Salmon, C. T., & Lee, J. S. (1983). Perceptions of newspaper fairness: A structural approach. *Journalism Quarterly, 60*(4), 663-676.

Schmermund, G. (1986). Interview.

Schneider, L. A. (1985a). The role of public relations in four organizational types. *Journalism Quarterly, 62*(3), 567-576, 594.

Schneider, L. A. (1985b). *Organizational structure, environmental niches, and public relations: The Hage-Hull typology of organizations as predictor of communication behavior.* Doctoral dissertation, University of Maryland, College Park.

Schneider, L. A. (1985c). Implications of the concept of the schema for public relations. *Public Relations Research & Education, 2*(2), 36-47.

Schwartz, D. F. (1986). *A systems theory view of organizations as communication networks.* Paper presented at the meeting of the International Communication Association, Chicago.

Scrimger, J. (1985). Profile: Women in Canadian public relations. *Public Relations Review, 11*(3), 40-46.

Scriven, M. (1967). The methodology of evaluation. In R. W. Tyler, R. M. Gagne, & M. Scriven (Eds.), *Perspectives of curriculum evaluation* (pp. 39-83). AERA Monograph Series on Curriculum Evaluation 1. Chicago: Rand McNally.

Selnow, G. W., & Wilson, S. (1985). Sex roles and job satisfaction. *Public Relations Review, 11*(4), 38-47.

Sethi, P. (1983). Institutional/image advertising and idea/issue advertising as marketing tools: Some public policy issues. *Journal of Marketing, 47*(1), 68-78.

Shaw, D., & McCombs, M. (1977). *The emergence of American political issues: the agenda-setting function of the press.* St.Paul, MN: West.

Shelby, A. N. (1984). *Issues management survey.* Unpublished paper.

Shelby, A. N. (1986). *Issues management: A new direction for public relations professionals.* Paper presented at the meeting of the International Communication Association, Chicago.

Sherrell, D., Reidenbach, R. E., Moore, E., Wagle, J., & Spratlin, T. (1985). Exploring consumer response to negative publicity. *Public Relations Review, 11*(1), 13-28.

Sjoberg, G., & Nett, R. (1968). *A methodology for social research.* New York: Harper & Row.

Skinner, R. W., & Shanklin, W. L. (1978). The changing role of public relations in business firms. *Public Relations Review, 4*(2), 40-45.

Smith, D. R., & Rabin, K. H. (1978). What broadcasters want in public service spots. *Public Relations Review, 4*(10), 29-36.

Smith, K. A. (1984). Perceived influence of media on what goes on in a community. *Journalism Quarterly, 61*(2), 260-264.

Smith, T. W. (1980). America's most important problem: A trend analysis, 1946-1976. *Public Opinion Quarterly, 44*(2), 164-180.

Snyder, L. (1978). Uses and gratifications to implement a public relations program. *Public Relations Journal, 4*(2), 32-39.

Snyder, L. (1983). An anniversary review and critique of the Tylenol crisis. *Journalism Quarterly, 60*(3), 24-34.

Sobel, J. L. (1982). Public health agenda-setting: Evaluation of a cardiovascular risk reduction campaign. Doctoral dissertation, University of Minnesota, Minneapolis.

Sohn, A. B. (1978). A longitudinal analysis of local non-political agenda-setting effects. *Journalism Quarterly, 55*(2), 325-333.

Stamm, K. R. (1972). Environment and communication. In F. G. Kline & P. J. Tichenor (Eds.), *Current perspectives in mass communication research.* Newbury Park, CA: Sage.

Stamm, K. R. (1981). Measurement decisions. In G. H. Stempel III & B. H. Westley (Eds.), *Research methods in mass communication* (pp. 87-104). Englewood Cliffs, NJ: Prentice-Hall.

Stamm, K. R., & Grunig, J. E. (1977). Communication situations and cognitive strategies in resolving environmental issues. *Journalism Quarterly, 54*(4), 713-720.

Stanford, S., & Riccomini, B. (1984). *Linking TV programs' orientations and gratifications: An experimental approach. Journalism Quarterly, 61*(1), 76-82.

St. Dizier, B. (1985). The effect of newspaper endorsements and party identification on voting choice. *Journalism Quarterly, 62*(3). 589-594.

Stephens, L. F. (1981). Professionalism of army public affairs personnel. *Public Relations Review, 7*(2), 43-56.

Stephens, M., & Edison, N. G. (1982). News media coverage of issues during the accident at Three-Mile Island. *Journalism Quarterly, 59*(2), 199-204.

Stevens, R. (1984). Twentieth annual survey of the profession, part I. *PR Reporter 27,* 40.

Stevens, R. (1985). Twenty-first annual survey of the profession, part I: Salaries. *PR Reporter 28,* 30.

Stevenson, R. L. (1979). Use of public television by blacks. *Journalism Quarterly, 56*(1), 141-147.

Stocking, S. H. (1985). Effects of public relations efforts on media visibility of organizations. *Journalism Quarterly, 62*(2), 358-366.

Stone, G. C. (1976). Communication study could use more emphasis. *Public Relations Review, 2*(1), 11-21.

Stone, G. C., & McCombs, M. (1981). Tracing the time lag in agenda-setting. *Journalism Quarterly, 7*(1), 51-55.

Strand, P. J., Dozier, D. M., Hofstetter, C. R., & Ledingham, J. D. (1983). Campaign messages, media usage and types of voters. *Public Relations Review, 9*(4), 53-63.

Strasser, J. A. (1978). How to communicate with your scientific identity. *Public Relations Journal, 34*(10), 15-16.

Strenski, J. B. (1975). Problems in international public relations. *Public Relations Journal, 31*(5), 27-29.

Strenski, J. B. (1982). Communication audit useful for measuring public relations effectiveness. *Public Relations Quarterly, 27*(1), 22.

Surlin, S. H., & Walker, B. (1975). Employee evaluations of handling of news by a corporate newspaper. *Journalism Quarterly, 52*(1). 99-105.

Teahan, F. H. (1982). 1980 graduates: Where did they go? what did they earn? *Public Relations Journal, 38*(2), 12-13.

Tennant, F. A. (1978). Survey on licensing public relations practitioners. *Public Relations Review, 4*(1), 37-42.

Theus, K. T. (1985). Gender shifts in journalism and public relations. *Public Relations Review, 11*(1), 42-50.

Thompson, W. L. (1986). Interview.

Tichenor, P. J., Donohue, G. A., & Olien, C. N. (1977). Community research and evaluating community relations. *Public Relations Review, 3*(4), 96-109.

Tichenor, W. L., Donohue, G. A., Olien, C. N., & Bowers, J. K. (1971). Environment and public opinion. *Journal of Environmental Education, 2,* 38-42.

Tichenor, W. L., Nnaemeka, A. I., Olien, C. N., & Donohue, G. A. (1977). Community pluralism and perceptions of television content. *Journalism Quarterly, 54*(2), 254-261.

Towers, Perrin, Foster and Crosby, Inc. (1984). Not-for-profit compensation. *Public Relations Journal, 40*(5), 23-26.

Trujillo, N., & Toth, E. L. (1986). *Organizational paradigms for public relations research and practice.* Paper presented at the meeting of the Association for Education in Journalism and Mass Communication, Norman, OK.

Tunstall, J. (1977). *The media are American.* New York: Columbia University Press.

Turk, J. V. (1985). Information subsidies and influence. *Public Relations Review, 11*(3), 10-25.

Turk, J. V. (1986). *The status of public relations careers: Roles, games, mentoring and gender comparisons.* Paper presented at the meeting of the International Communication Association, Chicago.

Turow, J., & Park, C. (1981). TV publicity outlets: A preliminary investigation. *Public Relations Review, 7*(3), 15-24.

University of Florida, College of Journalism and Communications. (1983, May 27). *Issues management survey summary report.* Gainesville: Author.

University of Minnesota. (1979). Report. In General Motors Business Understanding Program, *Business and the news media: What are the roles of each?* Detroit, MI: General Motors.

Vanden Bergh, B., Fletcher, A. D., & Adrian, M. A. (1984). Local business press: New phenomenon in the news marketplace. *Journalism Quarterly, 61*(3), 645-649.

Van Leuven, J. K. (1980). Measuring values through public opinion. *Public Relations Review, 6*(1), 51-56.

Van Leuven, J. K. (1986). *A planning matrix for message design, channel selection and scheduling.* Paper presented at the the meeting of the Association for Education in Journalism and Mass Communication, Norman, OK.

Van Meter, J. (1984). Editorial services. In B. Cantor & C. Burger (Eds.), *Experts in action: Inside public relations* (pp. 196-203). New York: Longman.

Vaugh, D. K. (1982). Interview.

Wackman, D. B., Salmon, C. T., & Salmon, C. (1987). Developing an advertising agency-client relationship. *Journal of Advertising Research 26*: 21-28.

Walker, A. (1976). Education survey: Few changes, much growth. *Public Relations Review, 2*(1), 22-30.

Walker, A. (1982). End-of-decade survey shows academic growth in public relations. *Public Relations Review, 8*(2), 46-60.

Walker, A. (1984). Public relations education: 1983 survey and report. *Public Relations Review, 10*(1), 18-29.

Ward, S., Wackman, D. B., & Wartella, E. (1977). *How children learn to buy.* Newbury Park, CA: Sage.

Watt, J. H., Jr., & Vanden Berg, S. (1981). How time dependency influences media effects in a community controversy. *Journalism Quarterly, 58*(1), 43-50.

Weaver, D., & Elliot, S. N. (1985). A study of local agenda-building. *Journalism Quarterly, 62*(1), 87-94.

Weaver, R. A., & Glasser, T. L. (1984). Survey research for legislative relations. *Public Relations Review, 10*(1), 39-48.

Weis, R. J., & Stamm, K. R. (1984). Predictors of organizational newspaper use: A "community perspective." *Public Relations Research and Education, 1*(2), 4-14.

Weiss, C. H. (1972). *Evaluation research: Methods of assessing program effectiveness.* Englewood Cliffs, NJ: Prentice-Hall.

White, T. H. (1973). *The making of the president 1972.* New York: Atheneum.

Wilcox, D. L. (1979). Hiring criteria of public relations employers. *Public Relations Review, 5*(2), 35-42.

Williams, W., Jr., & Larson, D. C. (1977). Agenda-setting in an off-election year. *Journalism Quarterly, 54*(4), 744-749.

Williams, W., Jr., Shapiro, M., & Cutbrith, C. (1983). The impact of campaign agendas on perceptions of issues in 1980 campaign. *Journalism Quarterly, 60*(2), 226-231.

Wilson, C. E., & Howard, D. M. (1978). Public perception of media accuracy. *Journalism Quarterly, 55*(1), 73-76.

Wilson, J. Q. (1973). Planning and politics: Citizen participation in urban renewal. In R. L. Warren (Ed.), *Perspectives on the American community* (2nd ed., chap. 31). Chicago: Rand McNally.

Wimmer, R. D., & Dominick, J. R. (1983). *Mass media research.* Belmont, CA: Wadsworth.

Wollan, J. (1986). Interview.

Woolward, I. (1982, February). Advertising to the convertibles. *Madison Avenue,* pp. 30-32.

Wright, D. K. (1976). Social responsibility and public relations: A multi-step theory. *Public Relations Review, 2*(3), 24-36.

Wright, D. K. (1979). Professionalism and social responsibilty in public relations. *Public Relations Review, 5*(2), 20-33.

Wright, D. K. (1981). Accreditation's effects on professionalism. *Public Relations Review, 7*(1), 48-61.

Wright, D. K. (1982). Public relations education and the business schools. *Public Relations Review, 8*(2), 11-16.

Wright, D. K. (1983). Men, women and social responsibility. *Public Relations Journal, 39*(8), 27-29.

Wright, D. K. (1985). Age and the moral values of practitioners. *Public Relations Review, 11*(1), 51-60.

Wylie, F. W. (1975). Attitudes toward the media. *Public Relations Journal, 31*(1), 6-7.

Zhao, X., & Chaffee, S. H. (1986). *Political ads vs. news as sources of issue information.* Paper presented at the meeting of the Association for Education in Journalism and Mass Communication, Norman, OK.

Zotti, E. (1985). Thinking psychographically. *Public Relations Journal, 41(5), 26-30.*

INDEX

ABOUT THE AUTHOR

JOHN V. PAVLIK is Assistant Professor of Communications in the School of Communications, The Pennsylvania State University, University Park, PA. He has recently developed a course in PR problems, which focuses largely on applications of PR research to case problems in public relations. He has also developed a new course in PR research. He has published articles in *Public Relations Review* and *Public Relations Research and Education*. His articles include "Employee Communications: A Uses and Gratifications Approach to Employee Newsletter Readership" and "Theoretic Approaches in Public Relations Research." He serves on the editorial review board for *Public Relations Research and Education*. He also served for two years as the assistant to the editor for *Communication Research*. He has published computer software for instruction in PR, journalism, advertising, and media studies. He is also on the software editorial review board for the Oates Clearinghouse, Miami, FL. In 1983, he received his doctoral degree in mass communication from the University of Minnesota, where he also received his master's degree in 1980. Before pursuing graduate studies, he worked in the PR department at American Family Insurance Group, Madison, WI.